Selected Poems of Ben Jonson

Edited by

Ted-Larry Pebworth

and

Claude J. Summers

MEDIEVAL & RENAISSANCE TEXTS & STUDIES
Binghamton, New York
1995

© Copyright 1995
Center for Medieval and Early Renaissance Studies
State University of New York at Binghamton

Library of Congress Cataloging-in-Publication Data

Jonson, Ben, 1573?–1637.
    [Poems. Selections]
    Selected poems of Ben Jonson / edited by Ted-Larry Pebworth and
Claude J. Summers.
        p.   cm. — (Pegasus paperbooks)
    Includes bibliographical references and index.
    ISBN 0–86698–178–0 (pbk.: alk. paper)
    I. Pebworth, Ted-Larry. II. Summers, Claude J. III. Title.
PR2602.P43 1995
821'.3—dc20   95–8284
                                                                  CIP

Printed in the United States of America

For
Mary Ann & Gary Stringer

PERFECT IN A CIRCLE ALWAYES MEET

Contents

Chronology	vi
Introduction	ix
Selected Bibliography	xv
A Note on the Text and Commentary	xvii
Selections from *Epigrammes*	1
The Forrest	23
Selections from *The Under-Wood*	48
"To the memory of ... *William Shakespeare*"	81
Index of Titles and First Lines	85

Chronology

1573 (?)   Ben Jonson born, probably in or near London, 11 June (?), one month after the death of his father, a minister of the Church of England.

1574–1583   Jonson's mother marries a master bricklayer living in Westminster. Jonson attends a school attached to St. Martin-in-the-Fields Church.

1583–1588   Attends Westminster School, studies with William Camden, who was to become one of his age's greatest classicists, antiquarians, and teachers.

1588–1596   Apprenticed as a bricklayer to his stepfather. Serves briefly as a volunteer soldier in Flanders.

1594   Marries Anne Lewis of the parish of St. Magnus the Martyr, London, 14 November. Almost nothing is known of Jonson's wife except his 1619 description of her as "a shrew yet honest."

1597   Acts in a strolling company of players. Employed by the Admiral's Men as a playwright. Collaborates on *The Isle of Dogs* (now lost), a play found objectionable by Queen Elizabeth's Privy Council: Jonson and two of the actors briefly imprisoned for sedition.

1598   Obtains the "freedom" of the Company of Tilers and Bricklayers, thus becoming a journeyman of the craft. *The Case Is Altered* performed by the Children of the Chapel Royal. *Every Man in His Humour* performed by the Lord Chamberlain's Men in mid-September. Kills a fellow actor, Gabriel Spencer, in a duel, 22 September; imprisoned in Newgate, and freed on a plea of right of clergy, but branded on the thumb and his goods confiscated. While in prison, visited and converted by a Roman Catholic priest.

1599   Resumes collaborative writing for the Admiral's Men. John Marston's satiric portrait of Jonson in *Histriomastix* sparks the War of the Theaters. *Every Man out of His Humour* performed late in the year by the Lord Chamberlain's Men.

1600	*Cynthia's Revels* performed late in the year by the Children of Queen Elizabeth's Chapel. *Every Man out of His Humour* published in quarto, inaugurating Jonson's practice—highly unusual for the day—of publishing his plays under careful authorial supervision.
1602–1607	Leaves his wife; lives with Esmé Stuart, Lord Aubigny.
1603	Queen Elizabeth dies, James I succeeds her. Begins era of Jonson's "entertainments" and court masques. His son Benjamin dies. *Sejanus* acted by the King's Men and hissed off the stage. Forms "The Mermaid Club," a drinking society for poets and wits.
1605	Voluntarily joins Marston and George Chapman, his collaborators on *Eastward Ho!*, in jail for mockery of the Scots.
1606	*Volpone* produced by the King's Men. Jonson and his wife charged for failure to take Anglican communion.
1607	Expressing satisfaction that *Volpone* was favorably regarded at "The Two Famous Universities," Jonson dedicates the quarto publication of the play to Oxford and Cambridge.
1608	Returns to the Church of England.
1609	*Epicoene* produced by the Children of Her Majesty's Revels.
1610	*The Alchemist* acted by the King's Men.
1611	*Catiline* produced by the King's Men.
1612–1613	Travels in France as tutor to the son of Sir Walter Ralegh.
1614	*Bartholomew Fair* performed by the Lady Elizabeth's Men.
1616	Publishes a folio edition of *Workes,* including nine plays, *Epigrammes, The Forrest,* and several masques and entertainments. *The Devil Is an Ass* acted by the King's Men. Granted a royal pension, recognition of his role as London's leading man of letters.
1616–1625	Presides over meetings of the "Tribe of Ben," a group of younger poets and wits who looked to Jonson as father-figure and teacher. The informal group meets at various London drinking establishments, including the Apollo Room of the Devil Tavern.
1618–1619	Makes a walking tour of Scotland, where he is entertained lavishly in Edinburgh and elsewhere; visits William Drummond of Hawthornden, a wealthy Scottish poet who kept notes on the famous poet's conversations during the visit.

1619	Awarded an honorary M.A. by Oxford University.
1623	Jonson's house and library destroyed by fire. Contributes poems to the first folio collection of Shakespeare's plays, a volume whose publication he encouraged.
1625	King James dies; Charles I succeeds him. Jonson's prestige at court declines.
1626	*The Staple of News* performed by the King's Men.
1628	Partially paralyzed by a stroke. Appointed Chronologer of the City of London.
1629	*The New Inn,* "most negligently play'd" by the King's Men, hissed by the audience.
1632	*The Magnetic Lady* performed by the King's Men.
1633	*A Tale of a Tub*, revised from an early draft, presented by Queen Henrietta's Men.
1637	Dies August 6. Buried three days later in Westminster Abbey. The epitaph "O rare Ben Jonson" carved into his blue marble grave stone.
1638	Publication of *Jonsonus Virbius*, a collection of commemorative verse in Jonson's honor.
1640–1641	Sir Kenelm Digby publishes the *Workes* in two folio volumes.

Introduction

Ben Jonson ranks among the most significant figures in English literature. A prolific writer who attempted most of the major poetic and dramatic genres of the seventeenth century, he is best known as a comic dramatist, the author of *Volpone* and *The Alchemist*. But Jonson is also the author of other superb comedies, two tragedies, a host of masques, and a large canon of excellent poetry. He wrote both for the popular stage and for the court, investing with intellectual substance and ethical dignity the elaborate spectacles favored by King James I. The diversity of his canon is only the most obvious instance of his resistance to neat categorization. A learned neoclassicist, he was also the master of coarse jests and earthy humor. He was both a felon convicted for slaying an actor in a duel and the arbiter of civilized values for the ruling class of his society. The step-son of a bricklayer, he became the defender of aristocratic privilege; the most urban of poets, who lived almost his entire life in London, he also idealized and mystified rural life. In his work he alternately portrayed the men and women of his age as gross and vulgar beasts and as reincarnations of ancient grace. But what animated—and unified—all of Jonson's diverse work, from his satiric epigrams to his love lyrics, were an abiding vision of human possibilities and an unflagging conviction of the true utility of poetry.

When King James awarded Jonson a pension in 1616, he became unofficially Poet Laureate of England, a position peculiarly appropriate for him because he is preeminently (though not exclusively) a public poet. His role as a social poet, in fact, helps distinguish him from his great contemporary John Donne. Together Jonson and Donne created a new kind of poetry in the late sixteenth- and early seventeenth-century, one characterized by their proclivity for the "plain style" of strong lines, colloquial language, natural rhythms, and economy of expression. Reacting against the sensuous ornateness and pictorial diffuseness of their Elizabethan predecessors and neo-Spenserian contemporaries, they created distinct and personal voices. Perhaps most influenced by the example of Sir Philip Sidney, their poetry is an intellectual, tough-minded verse in which the formal properties of rhythm and meter emphasize meaning; individual poems are organic, each part governed by a prior conception of the final form and growing into a highly structured, precisely crafted whole.

Donne and Jonson, who jointly influenced most of the seventeenth-century poets who followed them, differ chiefly and most clearly in that the former is more often a private poet. Introverted and sometimes eccentrically, unclassically individual, Donne is more intent on fashioning realms of private emotion than on creating a poetic commonwealth. Consequently, his poetry is more arcane and more often inaccessible than Jonson's; he writes more frequently of such private subjects as sex and religion; and he disdains print, remaining an amateur rather than a professional poet. He characteristically devises elaborate and extended conceits, self-consciously affecting wit and worrying minute points of (pseudo)logic and learning in order to startle his coterie readers into recognition and acquiescence. In contrast, Jonson is not as interested in discovering unexpected resemblances between unlike phenomena. While he is a far better love poet than is generally recognized, love is not his foremost poetic subject, and only once—in "To Heaven" (F-15)—does he approach a religious question with an intensity comparable to Donne's. Even when he is at his most personal—mourning his children, for instance—Jonson is never idiosyncratic, and he rarely attempts to capture the kind of emotional transport that Donne achieves in his verse.

Jonson does, however, incorporate space for the private emotions in his poetic commonwealth, and his love poetry characteristically utilizes a secrecy motif that intensifies its sense of intimacy. Moreover, unlike Donne, he is a professional writer who earned his living from his pen and pioneered in adapting to the period's emerging print culture, utilizing it to create and fix his canon and individual texts as unchanging and unchangeable artifacts. As the first major poet so involved in the printing of his work—especially the folio *Workes* of 1616—Jonson had a major impact on his contemporaries and following generations of poets. His practice stimulated among them a recognition of the control made available by print transmission and, in effect, created the conditions under which literary study and systematic criticism could flourish. Not only did the 1616 folio establish Jonson as the leading man of letters in London, it also constituted a daring claim for the permanent value of vernacular literature.

Jonson's role as social poet is a function of his vaunted classicism. Although he was not educated at either of the two English universities, he became a formidable classical scholar. The classical qualities in Jonson's poetry may be located in a number of specific manifestations, including the urbanity, (deceptive) simplicity, and decorum of his lyrics, his self-conscious identification with poets like Martial and Horace, and his embrace of such classical ideals as balance and self-sufficiency. In addition, Jonson revives classical forms such as the epigram, the epitaph, the ode, the epode, and the verse epistle, and he does so with a scholar's knowledge of the origins and conventions of each genre. But the most fundamental reflection of his classicism is the social and public nature of his poetry, including his assumption of the poet's role as arbiter of civilized values. Jonson's entanglement in the elaborate and frequently treacherous patronage system of the day complicated his performance as counselor to the ruling classes. Nevertheless, much of his poetry is didactic, concerned with how best to achieve a good society, inspiring through praise and shaming through ridicule.

Jonson is seldom ecstatic and rarely does he create poems of private sensation. Nevertheless, there is a great deal of emotion in his verse. He is capable of conveying fine shades of feeling and of orchestrating delicate shifts of tone. From poem to poem he assumes a variety of dramatic poses, each of them true to one or another facet of his complex personality, and all of them invested with individualized emotion. He is tactful advisor, respectful admirer, proud poet, grieving father, courteous host, affectionate parodist, enraged satirist, amused observer, witty commentator, loving friend, loyal subject, unhandsome lover. Most often the persona he presents is characterized by enormous dignity and fierce independence, and sometimes he exposes himself as affectingly vulnerable. Nearly always, Jonson surfaces in his poetry as a man very much aware of the precariousness of his social and professional status within a harshly competitive society.

At first glance, the bulk of Jonson's verse may seem somewhat prosaic in its lack of startling imagery, its sparseness, and apparent straightforwardness. But while Jonson aims for clarity and artful shapeliness in his poetry, his "plain style" actually cloaks a great deal of ambivalence and ambiguity. Indeed, the very placidity of his surfaces often makes possible surprising and resonant reverberations. Jonson's poetry is active, animated by verbs rather than adjectives; it typically reinvigorates tired conventions and exhausted traditions; it is sometimes inventive, playful, and imaginative; and it is nearly always carefully controlled and neatly unified.

Jonson's poetry is especially distinguished by its precise diction and semantic play, as when he chooses a single word or phrase that echoes with implications. For instance, near the end of his famous tribute to the Sidney family, "To Penshurst" (F-2), he remarks that the Sidney children, by observing their parents, may learn "The mysteries of manners, armes, and arts." The word "mysteries," suggesting as it does a whole wealth of meaning, from secret social rites to the Christian religion itself, gives transcendence to what might appear merely a conventional compliment. Similarly, at the end of this poem, Jonson contrasts the owners of ostentatious prodigy houses with the owner of Penshurst: "their lords have built, but thy lord dwells." Deriving naturally from all that has gone before in the poem, this simple but precise opposition of building and dwelling implies a wealth of meaning, much of it suggestive rather than specific, but all of it appropriate to the central distinction between the imposing "heaps" erected for the sake of vanity and the organic, living embodiment of ancient values that is Penshurst.

But perhaps even more important than the verbal and linguistic skill of the poet is the tension he generates through the balancing of various oppositions throughout his work. He sometimes, as in "An Elegie" (U-22), depicts idealized landscapes only to have realistic figures intrude upon them, allowing experience to impinge upon innocence and realism to temper idealism. Often Jonson juxtaposes one emotion with another, as in "My Picture left in *Scotland*" (U-9), where playful wit balances and then intensifies pathos. Sometimes he places contradictory attitudes in opposition and refuses to reconcile them. "On My First Daughter" (E-22), for example, gains great power by never reconciling its opposition of soul and body, earth and heaven, allowing them to exist as discrete elements in the paradox of human love. Sometimes, Jonson mingles seemingly incongruous emotions without ever permitting them to develop into opposition, as in the "Epitaph on S[alomon] P[avy]" (E-120), where he is at once witty and sincere, playful and earnest. Jonson is a great dramatic poet: he not only assumes a variety of poses and creates vivid dramatic situations but he also orchestrates mood and tone and articulates implied and explicit dramatic contexts. His effects are often subtle; and his subtlety is itself a significant element of his craftsmanship.

This edition of Jonson's poetry presents selections from Jonson's *Epigrammes*, *The Forrest* in its entirety, selections from *The Under-Wood*, and Jonson's tribute to Shakespeare.

Jonson seems to have prepared his *Epigrammes* for publication in 1612, when it was entered in the Stationers' Register, but it apparently was not printed until its inclusion in Jonson's 1616 folio *Workes*. In dedicating them to William Herbert, earl of Pembroke, Jonson refers to his epigrams as "the ripest of my studies," distinguishes them from the scurrilous lampoons which had come to be synonymous with the term *epigram,* and extends to Herbert "the honor of leading forth so many good, and great names (as my verses mention on the better part) to their remembrance with posteritie." Following Martial, Jonson thought of the epigram as a form admitting a wide variety of subject and feeling. In theory, no theme is too exalted and no feeling too intense to be treated in an epigram; in practice, Jonson rarely treats explicitly religious subjects, and the collection contains no love poems. He most often uses the genre to satirize the foibles of his fellows, to celebrate his king, to compliment the worthy (especially his patrons or prospective patrons), to perform the various rites of friendship, and to commemorate the loss of loved ones. In the collection, satiric and panegyric, comic and serious poems occur almost at random (though the satiric epigrams, which dominate the first half of the collection, recede in the second); but what unites the whole is an individual sensibility that sees the follies of his age and celebrates its ideals. The style of the epigrams is colloquial, the tone familiar and conversational. The poems benefit from being read aloud, and their heavy punctuation seems calculated to help the reader in this regard.

The Forrest first appeared in the 1616 folio *Workes* immediately following *Epigrammes*. Consisting of fifteen poems in various forms and concerning diverse subjects, it is very different from *Epigrammes* in size, range of contents, and the variety of its verse forms. The title alludes to the classical term *Sylva*, which was used to refer to collections of works in various genres. Interestingly, however, while Jonson's *Forrest* is diverse in subject matter, it is not merely a haphazard collection. Rather it is a complexly unified, dramatically coherent miscellany, united by virtue of recurrent themes and gestures. *The Forrest* includes some of Jonson's most famous and most admired poems.

The Under-wood was first published in the posthumous folio *Workes* of

1640–41, which was seen through the press by Jonson's friend Sir Kenelm Digby, who gained access to the manuscripts upon the poet's death in 1637. Jonson apparently planned to publish the collection in 1631, when he wrote a brief, apologetic preface referring to its contents as "these poems of later growth." The contents may be arranged in a rough chronological order: most of the first forty-two poems were probably written before Jonson's visit to Scotland in 1619, while the latter forty-six probably were composed after that date. The later works give eloquent testimony to Jonson's continuing power as a nondramatic poet throughout his life. Among the poems of *The Under-wood* are some of Jonson's finest and most ambitious efforts, such as the witty *tour de force* "A Celebration of CHARIS in ten Lyrick Peeces" (U-2) and the moving Pindaric ode "To the immortall memorie, and friendship of that noble paire, Sir *LUCIUS CARY*, and Sir *H. MORISON*" (U-70). In this final gathering Jonson continues to fulfill the social functions he accepted as his responsibility, but more frequently than in the earlier books he focuses upon himself as a unique and vulnerable individual.

The selection concludes with Jonson's poem, "To the memory of my beloved, The AUTHOR MR. WILLIAM SHAKESPEARE: AND what he hath left us." First published in the 1623 folio of Shakespeare's plays, collected by John Heminges and Henry Condell, actors in Shakespeare's company and friends of Jonson, the poem naturally integrates the two external factors that motivated it: the death of Shakespeare (in 1616) and the publication of his work. An enormously influential document in the history of Shakespeare's reputation, Jonson's tribute helped define the terms by which Shakespeare emerged as a national hero and a transcendent genius. Interestingly, Jonson imposes on his friend and sometime rival his own literary theories, perhaps in the process attempting to remake Shakespeare in Jonson's own image.

Jonson's idealism is rooted in his belief that poetry—that "dulcet, and gentle *Philosophy*, which leades us, and guides us by the hand to Action, with a ravishing delight, and incredible Sweetnes" (*Discoveries* 2398–2400)—was essential to the health of individuals and societies. Paraphrasing Cicero, he described poetry as an art which "nourisheth and instructeth our Youth; delights our Age; adornes our prosperity; comforts our Adversity; entertaines us at home; keepes us company abroad, travailes with us; watches, divides the times of our earnest, and sports; shares in our Country recesses and recreations; insomuch as the wisest and best learned have thought her the absolute Mistresse of manners and neerest of kin to Vertue" (*Discoveries* 2389–96). If he complained that *"Poetry,* in this latter Age, hath prov'd but a meane *Mistresse,* to such as have wholly addicted themselves to her" (*Discoveries* 622–24), his disillusionment was not with poetry but with his debased era. "An other Age, or juster men," he remained confident, "will acknowledge the vertues of [the poet's] studies: his wisdome, in dividing; his subtilty, in arguing: with what strength hee doth inspire his readers; with what sweetnesse hee strokes them: in inveighing, what sharpnesse; in Jest, what urbanity he uses" (*Discoveries* 786–91).

Demonstrating in his poetry those qualities that he expected posterity to value, Jonson looked to the future for that "legitimate fame" he sought from learned critics. His idealistic conception of the poet-priest was certainly not original with him, but he exemplified in his poetic practice the continuity of Orpheus's direct line.

Selected Bibliography

Blissett, William, Julian Patrick, and R. W. Van Fossen, eds. *A Celebration of Ben Jonson.* Toronto: Univ. of Toronto Press, 1973.

Evans, Robert C. *Ben Jonson and the Poetics of Patronage.* Lewisburg, Pa.: Bucknell Univ. Press, 1989.

Ferry, Anne. *All in War with Time: Love Poetry of Shakespeare, Donne, Jonson, Marvell.* Cambridge: Harvard Univ. Press, 1975.

Gardiner, Judith Kegan. *Craftsmanship in Context: The Development of Ben Jonson's Poetry.* The Hague: Mouton, 1975.

Helgerson, Richard. *Self-Crowned Laureates: Spenser, Jonson, Milton, and the Literary System.* Berkeley: Univ. of California Press, 1983.

Herendeen, W. H. and Jennifer Brady, eds. *Ben Jonson's 1616 Folio.* Newark: Univ. of Delaware Press, 1991.

Jonson, Ben. *Ben Jonson.* Ed. C. H. Herford and Percy and Evelyn Simpson. 11 vols. Oxford: Clarendon Press, 1925-52.

Judkins, David C. *The Non-Dramatic Works of Ben Jonson: A Reference Guide.* Boston: G. K. Hall, 1982.

Kernan, Alvin, ed. *Two Renaissance Mythmakers: Christopher Marlowe and Ben Jonson.* Baltimore: Johns Hopkins Univ. Press, 1977.

McCanles, Michael. *Jonsonian Discriminations: The Humanist Poet and the Praise of True Nobility.* Toronto: Univ. of Toronto Press, 1992.

Miner, Earl. *The Cavalier Mode from Jonson to Cotton.* Princeton: Princeton Univ. Press, 1961.

Nichols, J. G. *The Poetry of Ben Jonson.* New York: Barnes and Noble, 1969.

Parfitt, George A. E. *Ben Jonson: Public Poet, Private Man.* New York: Barnes and Noble, 1977.

Peterson, Richard S. *Imitation and Praise in the Poetry of Ben Jonson.* New Haven: Yale Univ. Press, 1981.

Riggs, David. *Ben Jonson: A Life.* Cambridge: Harvard Univ. Press, 1989.

Summers, Claude J. and Ted-Larry Pebworth. *Ben Jonson.* Twayne's English Authors Series 268. Boston: Twayne, 1979.

———., eds. *Classic and Cavalier: Essays on Jonson and the Sons of Ben.* Pittsburgh: Univ. of Pittsburgh Press, 1982.

Summers, Joseph H. *The Heirs of Donne and Jonson.* New York: Oxford Univ. Press, 1970.

Trimpi, Wesley. *Ben Jonson's Poems: A Study of the Plain Style.* Stanford: Stanford Univ. Press, 1962.

van den Berg, Sara. *The Action of Ben Jonson's Poetry.* Newark: Univ. of Delaware Press, 1987.
Wayne, Don E. *Penshurst: The Semiotics of Place and the Poetics of History.* Madison: Univ. of Wisconsin Press, 1984.
Wiltenberg, Robert. *Ben Jonson and Self-Love: The Subtlest Maze of All.* Columbia: Univ. of Missouri Press, 1990.

A Note on the Text and Commentary

Renaissance English poetry should be read, insofar as possible, in its original spelling and punctuation. To modernize spelling is to obscure what is often significant wordplay, such as is possible in the common Renaissance spellings "travail" for both "travail" and "travel" ("This man hath travail'd well"—E-128.14), "loose" for both "loose" and "lose" ("O, could I loose all father, now"—E-45.5), and "faine" for both "fain" and "feign" ("who could so exceed / *Nature*, they thought, in all, that he would faine"—E-79.7-8). To modernize spelling is also to lose the sight rhymes so obviously important to many poets of the period, among them Jonson, in whose poetry we find rome/home (F-4.66,68) stone/grone (F-2.45–46), Muse/chuse (E-109.1–2), world/horl'd (U-38.73–74), men/agen (U-41.21–22), and many other spellings for sight rhyme. In addition, Renaissance spelling may also offer important clues to pronunciation at the turn of the seventeenth century.

To modernize Renaissance punctuation is also inadvisable. It obscures and defeats the rhetorically based punctuation of the period. Although punctuation based on grammar was beginning to take hold in the late Renaissance, and Jonson makes a slight bow toward it in *The English Grammar,* the bulk of his remarks regarding punctuation in that handbook show that he saw pointing primarily as a rhetorical device, used to indicate the relative lengths of pauses between words and phrases when reading a work aloud. In general, he uses a comma to indicate a pause of one beat, a semicolon to indicate a pause of two beats, a colon to indicate a pause of three beats, and a period, question mark, or exclamation mark to indicate a pause of four beats.

Presenting Renaissance texts in their original spelling and punctuation can, of course, create problems for non-specialist readers. To relieve those problems as much as possible, we have glossed and annotated the poetry rather heavily. In particular, we have given modern spellings in the glosses when the originals might mislead the reader, as in then/than, to/too, bad/bade, past/passed, and mist/missed. At the same time, however, we have attempted to make the glossing and annotation as unintrusive as possible, so that the reader may ignore what he or she does not need. Our general rule has been to put as much of the annotation as possible on the line itself, to the right of the text, with the words or phrases being glossed or annotated marked with the symbol °. When the glosses and annotations could not be accommodated on the lines themselves, we have placed them at the bottoms of the pages, boldfacing the line numbers and the words being annotated (or the beginning and ending words in the case of phrases).

The citations *Discoveries* and *Conversations* used in the Introduction and the annotations refer, respectively, to Jonson's *Timber: or, Discoveries* and *Ben Jonson's Conversations with William Drummond of Hawthornden*, the former quoted from volume 8 of the Herford and Simpson edition (561–649), the latter from volume 1 (128–78). In each case, the line numbers cited are those supplied by Herford and Simpson.

The copy-texts for this edition are the corrected sheets of the following: *The Workes of Beniamin Jonson* (London: William Stansby, 1616) for *Epigrammes* and *The Forrest*; *The Workes of Benjamin Jonson. The second Volume* (London: for Richard Meighen, 1640) for *The Under-wood* (except for U-14); John Selden, *Titles of Honor* (London: William Stansby for Iohn Helme, 1614) for U-14; and *Mr. William Shakespeares Comedies, Histories, & Tragedies* (London: Isaac Iaggard and Ed. Blount, 1623) for S-2. The individual poems of *Epigrammes* and *The Forrest* are numbered, in roman, in their original publications. For ease of reference, we have silently converted those numbers to arabic and have prefaced them with "E" and "F," respectively. We have followed the editorially supplied numbering in the Herford and Simpson edition for the selections from *The Under-wood*, silently converting their roman numerals to arabic and prefacing each with "U"; and we have supplied an initial and number for the poem on Shakespeare. Although we have not modernized spelling, we have silently altered obsolete uses of *i/j*, *u/v*, *vv/w*, and the long *s* to reflect modern conventions of orthography. All other emendations are detailed below by poem and line numbers, with the copy-text readings following the right brackets:

E-92.14 twelve] twelves   17 lock'd] look'd   22 con' the] con'the
E-102.3 the good] be good

F-3.25 friends,] friends;   46 lent] lend
F-12.28 still] still,
F-13.123 finde;] finde?

Section heading THE UNDER-WOOD.] VNDER-VVOODS.
U-1.1.9 *sacrifice,*] *sacrifice.*   32 Of] of   34 Union] Unitie   41 Sanctifier,] Sanctifier.
U-1.2.1–32 *italics reversed*   12 sweet,] *sweet.*
U-1.3.1–24 *italics reversed*
U-2.2.19 looke;] looke,   22 with] which
U-2.3.4 limbes,] limbes;   more;] more   6 me:] me   9 Love] love   11 draught;] draught   25 doe,] doe
U-2.4.4 guideth;] guideth
U-2.5.23 in!] in?   50 spi'd.] spi'd
U-2.6.4 faire,] faire.
U-2.7.7 gone:] gone
U-2.9.5 me;] me.   9 I'ld] Il'd

U-2.10.6 understood:] understood
U-4.1–12 *italics reversed*
U-9.15 yeares,] yeares.
U-14.title ascription *omitted*] BEN: IONSON SELDEN.] SELDEN salutation *omitted*] H E A L T H.   25 it] it'   42 Blots and] Blots &   70 and] &
U-22.17 rear'd,] rear'd
U-38.7 it;] it,   16 me,] me   30 before;] before,   43 as] is   50 unjust;] unjust,   60 have!] have?   69 pardons] pardons,   74 skie,] skie;   78 die;] die   79 mornes,] mornes;   92 die,] die   105 Mistris] Masters
117 heart;] heart   121 have;] have,
U-40.9 me, Mistris,] me M$^{rs.}$ stealth,] stealth   20 rarified] ratified   spright;] spright   25 Mistris] Masters   38 belie] belie.   48 not] nor
U-41.2 Mistris] Masters   19 it:] it,   22 see] See
U-42.8 horse?] horse   21 not,] not   22 Wish] Wish,   44 force,] force.   47 Chaires] Chaires;   52 That] that
U-47.4 them not,] them, not   gold.] gold,   7 eyes,] eyes;   58 crack'd,] crack'd
U-49.12 theame?] theame.   25 Divine;] Divine
U-64.22 CHARLES,] CHARLES
U-70.68 bald] bold   91 long] Long
U-88.title *editorially supplied*] *The same translated.*

S-2.1–80 *italics reversed*   29 didst] *didstst*   40 Sent] *sent*   60 Such] *such*

Selected Poems of Ben Jonson

Selections from
EPIGRAMMES.

TO THE GREAT
EXAMPLE OF
HONOR AND
VERTUE,
THE MOST NOBLE
WILLIAM,
EARLE OF PEMBROKE,
L. CHAMBERLAYNE, &c.

MY LORD. *While you cannot change your merit, I dare not change your title: It was that made it, and not I. Under which name, I here offer to your Lo: the ripest of my studies, my* Epigrammes; *which, though they carry danger in the sound, doe not therefore seeke your shelter: For, when I made them, I had*
5 *nothing in my conscience, to expressing of which I did need a cypher. But if I be falne into those times, wherein, for the likenesse of vice, and facts, every one thinks anothers ill deeds objected to him; and that in their ignorant and guiltie mouthes, the common voyce is (for their securitie)* Beware the Poet, *confessing therein, so much love to their diseases, as they would rather make a partie for*
10 *them, then be either rid, or told of them: I must expect, at your Lo: hand, the protection of truth, and libertie, while you are constant to your owne goodnesse. In thankes whereof, I returne you the honor of leading forth so many good, and great names (as my verses mention on the better part) to their remembrance with posteritie. Amongst whom, if I have praysed, unfortunately, any one, that doth*
15 *not deserve; or, if all answere not, in all numbers, the pictures I have made of them: I hope it will be forgiven me, that they are no ill pieces, though they be not like the persons. But I foresee a neerer fate to my booke, then this: that the vices*

---

title] **WILLIAM ... PEMBROKE**: one of Jonson's patrons, William Herbert (1580–1630), third earl of Pembroke, Sir Philip Sidney's nephew and himself a poet; Jonson dedicated both *Catiline* and *Epigrammes* to him and each year received from him £20 to buy books (*Conversations* 312–13); Pembroke held several important offices in James's government; see E-102
2 *Lo:* Lordship
4 *sound*: name, reputation
5 *cypher*: hidden code
6 *falne*: fallen
9 *partie*: faction
10 *then*: than; *Lo:* Lordship's
17 *then*: than

therein will be own'd before the vertues (though, there, I have avoyded all particulars, as I have done names) and that some will be so readie to discredit
20   me, as they will have the impudence to belye themselves. For, if I meant them not, it is so. Nor, can I hope otherwise. For, why should they remit any thing of their riot, their pride, their selfe-love, and other inherent graces, to consider truth or vertue; but, with the trade of the world, lend their long eares against men they love not: and hold their deare Mountebanke, or Jester, *in farre better condition,*
25   *then all the studie, or studiers of* humanitie? *For such, I would rather know them by their visards, still, then they should publish their faces, at their perill, in my* Theater, *where* CATO, *if he liv'd, might enter without scandall.*

Your Lo: most faithfull honorer,

BEN. JONSON.

[E-1]   TO THE READER.

Pray thee, take care, that tak'st my booke in hand,
To reade it well: that is, to understand.

[E-2]   TO MY BOOKE.

It will be look'd for, booke, when some but see
    Thy title, *Epigrammes,* and nam'd of mee,
Thou should'st be bold, licentious, full of gall,
    Wormewood, and sulphure, sharpe, and tooth'd withall;°   *in addition*
5   Become a petulant thing, hurle inke, and wit,
    As mad-men stones: not caring whom they hit.
Deceive their malice, who could wish it so.
    And by thy wiser temper, let men know
Thou art not covetous of least selfe fame,
10   Made from the hazard of anothers shame:
Much lesse with lewd, prophane, and beastly phrase,
    To catch the worlds loose laughter, or vaine gaze.
He that departs with his owne honesty
    For vulgar° praise, doth it too dearely buy.   *common*

---

24 **Mountebanke**: charlatan
25 **then**: than
26 **visards**: masks; **then**: than
27 **CATO**: Roman statesman (234–149 BC) who attacked luxury, vice, and innovation; called the "conscience of Rome"
E-2.2 ***Epigrammes***: in Elizabethan England, epigrams had become synonymous with scurrilous lampoons (see E-18); **nam'd . . . mee**: bearing my name; Jonson was best known in 1616 as a satiric playwright

2

[E-3]   TO MY BOOKE-SELLER.

    Thou, that mak'st gaine thy end, and wisely well,
       Call'st a booke good, or bad, as it doth sell,
    Use mine so, too: I give thee leave. But crave
       For the lucks sake, it thus much favour have.
5 To lye upon thy stall, till it be sought;
       Not offer'd, as° it made sute° to be bought;   *as if/plea*
    Nor have my title-leafe on posts, or walls,
       Or in cleft-sticks,° advanced to make calls   *as placards*
    For termers, or some clarke-like° serving-man,   *clerk-like: scholarly*
10 Who scarse can spell th'hard names: whose knight lesse can.
    If, without these vile arts, it will not sell,
       Send it to *Bucklers-bury*, there 'twill, well.

[E-5]   ON THE UNION.

    When was there contract better driven by *Fate*?
       Or celebrated with more truth of state?
    The world the temple was, the priest a king,
       The spoused paire two realmes, the sea the ring.

[E-6]   TO ALCHYMISTS.

    If all you boast of your great art be true;
       Sure, willing povertie lives most in you.

E-3.7 title-leafe titlepage (as an advertisement)
9 termers: visitors to London
12 Bucklers-bury: a market in London, where pages of unsold books were used to wrap purchases
E-5.title] UNION: of England and Scotland under a single monarch; James VI of Scotland became James I of England in 1603; the two Parliaments were not combined, however, until the early eighteenth century
E-6.1 art: transmuting base metals into gold

[E-9]   TO ALL, TO WHOM I WRITE.

    May none, whose scatter'd names honor my booke,
        For strict degrees of ranke, or title looke:
    'Tis 'gainst the manners of an *Epigram:*
        And, I a *Poet* here, no *Herald* am.

[E-11]   ON SOME-THING, THAT WALKES SOME-WHERE.

    At court I met it, in clothes brave° enough,   *excellent, showy*
        To be a courtier; and lookes grave enough,
    To seeme a statesman: as I neere it came,
        It made me a great face, I ask'd the name.
5 A lord, it cryed, buried in flesh, and blood,
        And such from whom let no man hope least good,
    For I will doe none: and as little ill,
        For I will dare none. Good Lord, walke dead still.

[E-12]   ON LIEUTENANT SHIFT.°   *scheme, fraud*

    SHIFT, here, in towne, not meanest among squires,°   *pimps*
        That haunt *Pickt-hatch, Mersh-Lambeth,* and *White-fryers,*
    Keepes himselfe, with halfe a man, and defrayes
        The charge° of that state, with this charme, god payes.   *cost*
5 By that one spell he lives, eates, drinkes, arrayes
        Himselfe: his whole revennue is, god payes.
    The quarter day is come; the hostesse says,
        Shee must have money: he returnes, god payes.
    The taylor brings a suite home; he it 'ssayes,°   *assays: appraises*
10   Lookes o're the bill, likes it: and say's, god payes.
    He steales to ordinaries;° there he playes   *taverns*
        At dice his borrow'd money: which, god payes.
    Then takes up fresh commoditie, for dayes;
        Signes to new bond, forfeits: and cryes, god payes.
15   That lost, he keepes° his chamber, reades *Essayes,*   *keeps to*

E-9.4 **Herald**: an officer in charge of tracing and preserving genealogies of great families
E-11.8 **still**: playing with various meanings of the word: as yet, always, without motion
E-12.2 **Pickt-hatch ... White-fryers**: disreputable areas of London
3 **halfe a man**: emaciated manservant
4 **state**: manner of living; **charme**: magic incantation
6 **revennue**: accented on the second syllable
7 **quarter day**: that day each quarter when rents and other payments are due
13 **commoditie**: something bought on credit and immediately resold for cash
15 ***Essayes***: collections of short prose pieces usually written, in Jonson's day, on moral subjects; here contrasted with **Playes (17)**, the public performances of which were often accompanied by lewd behavior

4

      Takes physick,° teares the papers: still god payes.   *medicine*
    Or else by water goes, and so to playes;
      Calls for his stoole, adornes the stage: god payes.
    To every cause he meets, this voyce he brayes:
20   His onely answere is to all, god payes.
    Not his poore cocatrice° but he betrayes   *whore*
      Thus: and for his letcherie, scores, god payes.
    But see! th'old baud hath serv'd him in his trim,
      Lent him a pockie° whore. Shee hath paid him.   *syphilitic*

[E-14]   To William Camden.

    Camden, most reverend head, to whom I owe
      All that I am in arts, all that I know.
    (How nothings that?) to whom my countrey owes
      The great renowne, and name wherewith shee goes.
5   Then° thee the age sees not that thing more grave,   *than*
      More high, more holy, that shee more would crave.
    What name, what skill, what faith hast thou in things!°   *facts*
      What sight in searching the most antique springs!
    What weight, and what authoritie in thy speech!
10   Man scarse can make that doubt, but thou canst teach.
    Pardon free truth, and let thy modestie,
      Which conquers all, be once over-come by thee.
    Many of thine this better could, then° I,   *than*
      But for their powers, accept my pietie.°   *devotion*

[E-17]   To the Learned Critick.

    May others feare, flie, and traduce thy name,
      As guiltie men doe magistrates: glad I,

---

17 by . . . goes: is rowed across the Thames to the theaters located on the South Bank
18 stoole: would-be gallants paid to sit on stools on the stage itselt during dramatic performances, to be seen by all present
23 in . . . trim: in similar fashion; appropriately
E-14.title CAMDEN: noted antiquarian/historian (1551–1623) and one of Jonson's teachers at Westminster School
1 head: both headmaster at Westminster (after 1593) and Jonson's personal mentor throughout his career
3–4 countrey . . . name: Camden's *Britannia* (1586) and *Remaines of a Greater Worke concerning Britaine* (1605), each quickly running to several editions, popularized the ancient Roman name for England both at home and abroad
8 antique: pronounced "antic" with the accent on the first syllable
10 make . . . teach: ask a question before you can supply the answer
13 thine: your former students
14 for . . . powers: in the absence here of their greater abilities

5

> That wish my poemes a legitimate fame,
>   Charge them, for crowne, to thy sole censure hye.°   *hasten*
> 5 And, but a sprigge of bayes° given by thee,   *laurel*
>   Shall out-live gyrlands, stolne from the chast tree.

[E-18]   TO MY MEERE ENGLISH CENSURER.

> To thee, my way in *Epigrammes* seemes new,
>   When both it is the old way, and the true.
> Thou saist, that cannot be: for thou hast seene
>   DAVIS, and WEEVER, and the best have beene,
> 5 And mine come nothing like. I hope so. Yet,
>   As theirs did with thee, mine might credit get:
> If thou'ldst° but use thy faith, as thou didst then,   *thou wouldst*
>   When thou wert wont t'admire, not censure men.
> Pr'y thee° beleeve still, and not judge so fast,   *prithee: I pray thee*
> 10 Thy faith is all the knowledge that thou hast.

[E-22]   ON MY FIRST DAUGHTER.

> Here lyes to each her parents ruth,°   *grief, sorrow*
> MARY, the daughter of their youth:
> Yet, all heavens gifts, being heavens due,
> It makes the father, lesse, to rue.
> 5 At sixe moneths end, shee parted hence
> With safetie of her innocence;
> Whose soule heavens Queene,° (whose name shee beares)   *the Virgin Mary*
> In comfort of her mothers teares,
> Hath plac'd amongst her virgin-traine:°   *band of attendants*
> 10 Where, while that sever'd doth remaine,
> This grave partakes° the fleshly birth.   *partakes of, receives*
> Which cover lightly, gentle earth.

E-17.6 chast tree: the nymph Daphne was transformed into a laurel tree to escape the god Apollo's amorous pursuit; **chast**: chaste, with a pun on "chased"
E-18.title MEERE ENGLISH: who knows only English, in contrast to the learned critic of E-17
1 **my . . . new**: because they are not scurrilous lampoons (see E-2 and notes)
2 **old way**: in the classical tradition
4 **DAVIS . . . WEEVER**: authors of scurrilous epigrams; Sir John Davis of Hereford (1569–1626) published a collection about 1590, John Weever (1576–1632) published his *Epigrammes in the oldest cut, and newest fashion* in 1599
E-22: the dates of Mary Jonson's birth and death are unknown
10 **that . . . remaine**: her soul (already risen to Heaven) is separated from her body (the **"fleshly birth"** [11] left on earth) until the call to the Last Judgment, when the two will be reunited

[E-25]   ON SIR VOLUPTUOUS BEAST.

  While BEAST instructs his faire, and innocent wife,
   In the past pleasures of his sensuall life,
  Telling the motions of each petticote,°   *skirt*
   And how his GANIMEDE mov'd, and how his goate,
5 And now, her (hourely) her owne cucqueane° makes, *female cuckold*
   In varied shapes, which for his lust shee takes:
  What doth he else, but say, leave to be° chast,   *leave off being*
   Just wife, and, to change me, make womans hast.°   *haste*

[E-35]   TO KING JAMES.

  Who would not be thy subject, JAMES, t'obay
   A Prince, that rules by'example, more than sway?°   *power*
  Whose manners draw, more than thy powers constraine.
   And in this short time of thy happiest raigne,
5 Hast purg'd thy realmes, as° we have now no cause   *so that*
   Left us of feare, but first our crimes, then lawes.
  Like aydes 'gainst treasons who hath found before?
   And than in them, how could we know god more?
  First thou preserved wert, our king to bee,
10 And since, the whole land was preserv'd for thee.

[E-42]   ON GILES AND JONE.°   *Joan*

  Who sayes that GILES and JONE at discord be?
   Th'observing neighbours no such mood can see.
  Indeed, poore GILES repents he married ever.
   But that his JONE doth too. And GILES would never,
5 By his free will, be in JONES company.

E-25.4 GANIMEDE: the young Trojan lad taken to Olympus by Zeus to be his cupbearer and sexual plaything; more generally in the Renaissance, a boy kept for sexual purposes; **goate**: the ultimate symbol of lust

5 **hourely**: with a pun on "whorely"

5–6 **her owne ... takes**: he is unfaithful to his wife in having sexual intercourse with her when she is disguised as other women to whet his jaded appetite

8 **change me**: revive my (sexual) interest (in you)

E-35.4 this ... raigne: the poem was probably written no more than a year after James assumed the throne of England in 1603

5 **realmes**: Scotland and England

6 **lawes**: possibly a reference to the large number of new laws passed in March 1604

7 **treasons**: the unsuccessful plots against James by Gowry (1600) and by Cobham and Ralegh (1603)

10 **since ... thee**: referring to the plague of 1603, which delayed the new king's entry into London

      No more would JONE he should. GILES riseth early,
        And having got him out of doores is glad.
          The like is JONE. But turning home, is sad.
      And so is JONE. Oft-times, when GILES doth find
10   Harsh sights at home, GILES wisheth he were blind.
      All this doth JONE. Or that his long yearn'd life
        Were quite out-spun.° The like wish hath his wife.   *concluded*
      The children, that he keepes, GILES sweares are none
        Of his begetting. And so sweares his JONE.
15 In all affections shee concurreth still.°   *always*
      If, now, with man and wife, to will, and nill°   *not will*
        The selfe-same things, a note of concord be:
          I know no couple better can agree!

[E-43]   TO ROBERT EARLE OF SALISBURIE.

What need hast thou of me? or of my *Muse?*
    Whose actions so themselves doe celebrate?
Which should thy countries love to speak refuse,
    Her foes enough would fame thee in their hate.
5 'Tofore,° great men were glad of *Poets*: Now,   *heretofore*
    I, not the worst, am covetous of thee.
Yet dare not, to my thought, lest hope allow
    Of adding to thy fame; thine may to me,
When in my booke, men reade but CECILL's name,
10 And what I write thereof find farre, and free
From servile flatterie (common *Poets* shame)
    As thou stand'st cleere of the necessitie.

[E-45]   ON MY FIRST SONNE.

Farewell, thou child of my right hand, and joy;
    My sinne was too much hope of thee, lov'd boy,
Seven yeeres tho'wert° lent to me, and I thee pay,   *thou wert*
    Exacted by thy fate, on the just day.

E-42.11 long yearn'd: long-yarned, spun out to great length
E-43.title ROBERT ... SALISBURIE: Robert Cecil (1563–1612), created Earl of Salisbury on 4 May 1605; after the death of his father, Lord Burghley, he became the chief minister to Queen Elizabeth and prepared for the peaceful accession of King James to the throne of England
3–4 Which ... hate: which, if not spoken of, out of love, by your country would be made famous, out of hate, by her enemies
E-45.1 child ... hand: the boy (1596–1603) was named Benjamin, which in Hebrew means "child of the right hand" and implies both good fortune and dexterity; see Genesis 35:16–20

5   O, could I loose all father, now. For why
       Will man lament the state he should envie?
   To have so soone scap'd worlds, and fleshes rage,
       And, if no other miserie, yet age?
   Rest in soft peace, and ask'd, say here doth lye
10   BEN. JONSON his best piece of *poetrie.*
   For whose sake, hence-forth, all his vowes be such,
       As what he loves may never like too much.

[E-49]   TO PLAY-WRIGHT.

PLAY-WRIGHT me reades, and still° my verses damnes,	*always*
He sayes, I want° the tongue of *Epigrammes;*	*lack*

   I have no salt: no bawdrie he doth meane.
       For wittie, in his language, is obscene.
5   PLAY-WRIGHT, I loath to have thy manners knowne
       In my chast booke: professe them in thine owne.

[E-55]   TO FRANCIS BEAUMONT.

   How I doe love thee BEAUMONT, and thy *Muse,*

That unto me dost such religion° use!°	*faithfulness/exhibit*

   How I doe feare my selfe, that am not worth
       The least indulgent thought thy pen drops forth!
5   At once thou mak'st me happie, and unmak'st;
       And giving largely to me, more thou tak'st.
   What fate is mine, that so it selfe bereaves?
       What art is thine, that so thy friend deceives?
   When even there, where most thou praysest mee,
10   For writing better, I must envie thee.

---

5 **loose . . . father**: lose all sense of being a father, forget that I was ever a father
10 **BEN . . . his**: archaic form of "Ben Jonson's"; **best . . . poetrie**: with a play on the Greek root of "poet" as "maker"
E-49.title PLAY-WRIGHT: unidentified
3 **salt**: wit, with a pun on "salacious"
E-55.title FRANCIS BEAUMONT: a fellow poet and playwright (ca. 1584–1616), who wrote poems praising Jonson's *Volpone, Epicoene,* and *Catiline,* as well as a verse epistle addressed to Jonson, to which this epigram responds

[E-56]　　　　　　　　On Poet-Ape.

　　　Poore Poet-Ape, that would be thought our chiefe,
　　　　　Whose workes are eene° the fripperie° of wit,　　　*even/castoff clothing*
　　　From brocage° is become so bold a thiefe,　　　　　　*secondhand dealing*
　　　　　As we, the rob'd, leave° rage, and pittie it.　　　　*leave off, quit*
5　　At first he made low shifts, would picke and gleane,
　　　　　Buy the reversion of° old playes; now growne　　　*rights to*
　　　To'a little wealth, and credit in the *scene*,
　　　　　He takes up° all, makes each mans wit his owne.　　*steals*
　　　And, told of this, he slights it. Tut, such crimes
10　　The sluggish gaping auditor° devoures;　　　　　　　*audience member*
　　　　　He markes not whose 'twas first: and after-times
　　　May judge it to be his, as well as ours.
　　　　　Foole, as if halfe eyes will not know a fleece
　　　From locks of wooll, or shreds from the whole peece?

[E-59]　　　　　　　　On Spies.

　　　Spies, you are lights in state, but of base stuffe,
　　　Who, when you'have burnt your selves downe to the snuffe,
　　　Stinke, and are throwne away. End faire enough.

[E-62]　　　　　　　　To Fine Lady Would-bee.

　　　Fine Madame Would-bee, wherefore° should you feare,　　*why*
　　　　　That love to make so well, a child to beare?
　　　The world reputes you barren: but I know
　　　　　Your 'pothecarie, and his drug sayes no.
5　　Is it the paine affrights? that's soone forgot.
　　　　　Or your complexions losse? you have a pot,°　　　　*cosmetic jar*
　　　That can restore that. Will it hurt your feature?°　　　　*bodily appearance*
　　　　　To make amends, yo'are thought a wholesome creature.
　　　What should the cause be? Oh, you live at court:
10　　And there's both losse of time, and losse of sport
　　　　　In a great belly. Write, then on thy wombe,
　　　Of the not borne, yet buried, here's the tombe.

E-56.title POET-APE: a plagiarizing would-be poet playwright; unidentified
E-59.2 snuffe: the charred remnant of a candle wick
E-62.1–2 wherefore ... beare: why should you, who love to make a child (through sexual intercourse), fear to bear one?
4 drug: potion used to induce miscarriage

10

[E-65]   TO MY MUSE.

    Away, and leave me, thou thing most abhord
        That hast betray'd me to a worthlesse lord;
    Made me commit most fierce idolatrie
        To a great image through thy luxurie.°   *excess*
5 Be thy next masters more unluckie *Muse*,
        And, as thou'hast mine, his houres, and youth abuse.
    Get him the times long grudge, the courts ill will;
        And, reconcil'd, keepe him suspected still.°   *always*
    Make him loose all his friends; and, which is worse,
10   Almost all wayes, to any better course.°   *career*
    With me thou leav'st an happier *Muse* then° thee,   *than*
        And which thou brought'st me, welcome povertie.
    Shee shall instruct my after-thoughts to write
        Things manly, and not smelling° parasite.   *smelling of*
15 But I repent me: Stay. Who e're is rais'd,
        For worth he has not, He is tax'd, not prais'd.

[E-69]   TO PERTINAX° COB.°   *stiff/something big or stout*

    COB, thou nor° souldier, thiefe, nor fencer art,   *neither*
        Yet by thy weapon liv'st! Th'hast one good part.

[E-76]   ON LUCY COUNTESSE OF BEDFORD.

    This morning, timely rapt with holy fire,
        I thought to forme unto my zealous *Muse*,
    What kinde of creature I could most desire,
        To honor, serve, and love; as *Poets* use.°   *customarily do*
5 I meant to make her faire, and free, and wise,
        Of greatest bloud, and yet more good then° great;   *than*
    I meant the day starre should not brighter rise,
        Nor lend like influence from his lucent seat.
    I meant shee should be curteous, facile, sweet,
10   Hating that solemne vice of greatnesse, pride;
    I meant each softest vertue, there should meet,
        Fit in that softer bosome to reside.

E-65.9 **loose**: both let loose of (or reject) and lose
16 **tax'd**: obligated (to do better)
E-69.2 **by ... liv'st**: as a gigolo, a male prostitute
E-76.title **LUCY ... BEDFORD**: a noted aristocrat and courtier (1581?–1627), who patronized several poets, including Jonson and Donne
8 **lucent**: luminous, with a play on the name Lucy (from the Latin "lux": light, brightness)

        Onely a learned, and a manly soule
          I purpos'd her; that should, with even powers,
15   The rock, the spindle, and the sheeres controule
          Of destinie, and spin her owne free houres.
        Such when I meant to faine,° and wish'd to see,   *feign: imagine*
          My *Muse* bad,° *Bedford* write, and that was shee.   *bade*

[E-79]   To Elizabeth Countesse of Rutland.

        That *Poets* are far rarer births then° kings,   *than*
          Your noblest father prov'd: like whom, before,
        Or then, or since, about our *Muses* springs,°   *sources of inspiration*
          Came not that soule exhausted° so their store.   *that exhausted*
5   Hence was it, that the *destinies* decreed
          (Save that most masculine issue of his braine)
        No male unto him: who could so exceed
          Nature, they thought, in all, that he would faine.
        At which, shee happily displeas'd, made you:
10   On whom, if he were living now, to looke,
        He should those rare, and absolute numbers view,
          As he would burne, or better farre° his booke.   *make far better*

[E-89]   To Edward Allen.

        If *Rome* so great, and in her wisest age,
          Fear'd not to boast the glories of her stage,
        As skilfull Roscius, and grave Æsope, men,
          Yet crown'd with honors, as with riches, then;
5   Who had no lesse a trumpet of their name,

15–16 rock ... destinie: alluding to the three Parcæ, or Fates; the **rock** (distaff) of Clotho determined the moment of birth, the **spindle** of Lachesis spun the thread of life, and the **sheeres** of Atropos cut that thread
18 *Bedford* write: Lucy characteristically signed her letters with the boldly-written single word "Bedford"
E-79.title ELIZABETH ... RUTLAND: daughter (1584–1612) of Sir Philip Sidney, who fathered no **male (7)** children; see also F-12
6 most ... braine: probably referring to Sidney's prose romance *Arcadia*
8 faine: prefer, with a play on feign (imagine)
11 rare ... numbers: excellent poetry; referring to Elizabeth as her father's best piece of poetry (see E-14.10) or to poetry written by her; Jonson remarked to Drummond of Hawthornden that she "was nothing inferior to her Father ... in Poesie" (*Conversations* 213–14)
E-89.title EDWARD ALLEN: noted actor (1566–1626), who excelled in both tragic and comedic roles; partner, with his father-in-law Philip Henslowe, in the Fortune Theater; later proprietor of the Paris Bear Garden on the South Bank and founder of Dulwich College
3 ROSCIUS ... ÆSOPE: famous Roman actors of the first century BC, noted for comedy and tragedy, respectively

Then° CICERO, whose every breath was fame: *than*
   How can so great example dye in mee,
     That, ALLEN, I should pause to publish thee?
  Who both their graces in thy selfe hast more
10   Out-stript, then° they did all that went before: *than*
   And present worth in all dost so contract,
     As others speake, but onely thou dost act.
  Weare this renowne. 'Tis just, that who did give
     So many *Poets* life, by one should live.

[E-92]   THE NEW CRIE.

Ere cherries ripe, and straw-berries be gone,
   Unto the cryes° of *London* Ile° adde one; *of street vendors/I'll*
 Ripe statesmen, ripe: They grow in every street.
   At sixe and twentie, ripe. You shall'hem meet,
5 And have'hem yeeld no savour, but of state.
   Ripe are their ruffes, their cuffes, their beards, their gate,
 And grave as ripe, like mellow as their faces
   They know the states of *Christendome*, not the places:
 Yet have they seene the maps, and bought 'hem too,
10   And understand 'hem, as most chapmen° doe. *pamphlet sellers*
 The councels, projects, practises they know,
   And what each prince doth for intelligence owe,
 And unto whom: They are the almanacks
   For twelve yeeres yet to come, what each state lacks.
15 They carry in their pockets TACITUS,
   And the GAZETTI, or GALLO-BELGICUS:
 And talke reserv'd, lock'd up, and full of feare,
   Nay, aske you, how the day goes, in your eare.° *in a whisper*
 Keepe a *starre*-chamber sentence close,° twelve dayes: *secret*
20   And whisper what a Proclamation sayes.
 They meet in sixes, and at every mart,
   Are sure to con'° the catalogue° by hart; *memorize/published list*
 Or, every day, some one at RIMEE'S looks,
   Or BILS, and there he buyes the names of books.

---

6 CICERO: Roman orator and philosopher (106–43 BC), who praised Roscius and Æsope in *de Oratore* and *pro Sestio*
E-92.15 TACITUS: Roman historian (ca. 55–ca. 117), who wrote political histories of the early empire
16 GAZETTI: contemporaneous newssheets filled with as much speculation and gossip as fact; **GALLO-BELGICUS**: a notoriously inaccurate newssheet published in Cologne
19 *starre*-chamber: the criminal court of Star Chamber; Jonson implies that its sentences were always made public
23–24 RIMEE'S ... BILS: the well-known London bookshops of James Rime (or Rymer) and John Bill

25   They all get *Porta,* for the sundrie wayes
          To write in cypher, and the severall keyes,
     To ope' the character.° They'have found the sleight   *secret code*
          With juyce of limons, onions, pisse, to write.
     To breake up seales, and close 'hem. And they know,
30   If the *States*° make peace, how it will goe   *Low Countries*
          With *England.* All forbidden bookes they get.
     And of the poulder-plot, they will talke yet.
          At naming the *French* King, their heads they shake,
     And at the *Pope,* and *Spaine* slight faces make.
35   Or 'gainst the Bishops, for the Brethren,° raile,   *Puritan separatists*
          Much like those Brethren; thinking to prevaile
     With ignorance on us, as they have done
          On them: And therefore doe not onely shunne
     Others more modest, but contemne us too,
40   That know not so much state, wrong, as they doo.

[E-95]   TO SIR HENRIE SAVILE.

     If, my religion safe, I durst embrace
          That stranger doctrine of PYTHAGORAS,
     I should beleeve, the soule of TACITUS
          In thee, most weighty SAVILE, liv'd to us:
5   So hast thou rendred him in all his bounds,
          And all his numbers,° both of sense, and sounds.   *rhythms*
     But when I read that speciall piece, restor'd,
          Where NERO falls, and GALBA is ador'd,
     To thine owne proper° I ascribe then more;   *gift, ability*
10   And gratulate° the breach,° I griev'd° before: *praise/gap/lamented*
     Which *Fate* (it seemes) caus'd in the historie,
          Onely to boast thy merit in supply.
     O, would'st thou adde like hand, to all the rest!
          Or, better worke! were thy glad countrey blest,
15   To have her storie woven in thy thred;

---

25 ***Porta***: Giovanni Battista della Porta, whose book on writing in code was issued in 1563 and frequently reprinted
28 **juyce ... pisse**: liquids used instead of ink to write invisibly; the writing is made visible by heating the paper
29 **To ... 'hem**: to open and reseal letters without leaving traces
32 **poulder-plot**: the Gunpowder Plot, a thwarted attempt, allegedly by Roman Catholic conspirators, to blow up King James at the opening of Parliament, 5 November 1605
E-95.title **HENRIE SAVILE**: scholar (1549–1622), provost of Eton College, translator of Tacitus (see note to E-92.15); Savile supplied his own accounts of the end of the reign of **NERO** and the beginning of the reign of **GALBA (8)**, where Tacitus's original Latin texts had been lost
2 **doctrine ... PYTHAGORAS**: the transmigration of souls, reincarnation

14

MINERVAES loome was never richer spred.
For who can master those great parts like thee,
    That liv'st from hope, from feare, from faction free;
That hast thy brest so cleere of present crimes,
20   Thou need'st not shrinke at voyce of after-times;
Whose knowledge claymeth at the helme to stand;
    But, wisely, thrusts not forth a forward hand,
No more then° SALUST in the *Romane* state!   *than*
    As, then, his cause, his glorie emulate.
25 Although to write be lesser then° to doo,   *than*
    It is the next deed, and a great one too.
We need a man that knowes the severall graces
    Of historie, and how to apt° their places;   *make appropriate*
Where brevitie, where splendor, and where height,
30   Where sweetnesse is requir'd, and where weight;
We need a man, can speake of the intents,
    The councells, actions, orders, and events
Of state, and censure them: we need his pen
    Can write the things,° the causes, and the men.   *facts*
35 But most we need his faith (and all have you)
    That dares nor° write things false, nor hide things true.   *neither*

[E-96]   TO JOHN DONNE.

Who shall doubt, DONNE, where° I a *Poet* bee,   *whether*
    When I dare send my *Epigrammes* to thee?
That so alone canst judge, so'alone dost make:
    And, in thy censures, evenly, dost take
5 As free simplicitie, to dis-avow,
    As thou hast best authoritie, t'allow.
Reade all I send: and, if I find but one
    Mark'd by thy hand, and with the better stone,
My title's seal'd. Those that for claps° doe write,   *mass applause*
10   Let pui'nees,° porters, players praise delight,   *underlings*
And, till they burst,° their backs, like asses load: *break*
    A man should seeke great glorie, and not broad.

---

16 **MINERVAES loome**: Minerva was the Roman goddess of handicrafts, including weaving
23 **SALUST**: returning to Rome after a successful military career, Sallust (86–35 BC) declined to enter politics, preferring instead to devote himself to writing history
E-96.title JOHN DONNE: poet (1572–1631) and, after 1615, priest of the Church of England; Jonson told Drummond of Hawthornden that he "esteemeth John Done the first poet in the World in some things" but "that Done for not keeping of accent deserved hanging" and "that Done himself for not being understood would perish" (*Conversations* 117–18, 48–49, 196)
8 **better stone**: ancient Romans marked happy or successful days on their calenders with white stones

15

[E-101] INVITING A FRIEND TO SUPPER.

    To night, grave sir, both my poore house, and I
        Doe equally desire your companie:
    Not that we thinke us worthy such a ghest,
        But that your worth will dignifie our feast,
5   With those that come; whose grace may make that seeme
        Something, which, else, could hope for no esteeme.
    It is the faire acceptance, Sir, creates
        The entertaynment perfect: not the cates.°   *delicacies*
    Yet shall you have, to rectifie your palate,
10   An olive, capers, or some better sallade
    Ushring° the mutton; with a short-leg'd hen,   *preceding*
        If we can get her, full of egs, and then,
    Limons, and wine for sauce: to these, a coney°   *rabbit*
        Is not to be despair'd of, for our money;
15   And, though fowle, now, be scarce, yet there are clarkes,°   *scholars*
        The skie not falling, thinke we may have larkes.
    Ile tell you of more, and lye, so you will come:
        Of partrich, pheasant, wood-cock, of which some
    May yet be there; and godwit, if we can:
20   Knat, raile, and ruffe too. How so ere, my man°   *manservant*
    Shall reade a piece of VIRGIL, TACITUS,
        LIVIE, or of some better booke to us,
    Of which wee'll speake our minds, amidst our meate;
        And Ile professe° no verses to repeate: *vow, promise*
25   To° this, if ought appeare, which I know not of,   *in addition to*
        That will the pastrie, not my paper, show of.°   *appear by means of*
    Digestive cheese, and fruit there sure will bee;
        But that, which most doth take my *Muse,* and mee,
    Is a pure cup of rich *Canary*-wine,
30   Which is the *Mermaids,* now, but shall be mine:
    Of which had HORACE, or ANACREON tasted,
        Their lives, as doe their lines, till now had lasted.
    Tabacco, Nectar, or the *Thespian* spring,

E-101.19–20 **godwit . . . ruffe**: four kinds of edible birds found in marshes
21–22 **VIRGIL**: Roman poet (70–19 BC), author of the *Aeneid*; **TACITUS**: Roman historian especially admired by Jonson (see note to E-92.15); **LIVIE**: Roman historian (59 BC–AD 17)
26 **pastrie . . . of**: cooks of the period sometimes lined their baking pans with pages of unsold books; Jonson jokingly implies that some scraps of his poetry may appear on the table under a pie
29–30 ***Canary*-wine . . . *Mermaids***: a sweet white wine made in the Canary Islands, to be bought at the Mermaid, a noted London tavern of the period frequented by Jonson and his circle
31 **HORACE**: Roman poet (65–8 BC); **ANACREON**: Greek poet (6th century BC); Jonson especially admired and imitated both
33–34 ***Tabacco***: apparently sometimes brewed and drunk in the period; ***Nectar***: the drink of the Olympian gods; ***Thespian* spring**: on Mt. Helicon, sacred to the Muses; **LUTHERS**

        Are all but LUTHERS beere, to this I sing.
35   Of this we will sup free, but moderately,
        And we will have no *Pooly'*, or *Parrot* by;
    Nor shall our cups make any guiltie men:
        But, at our parting, we will be, as when
    We innocently met. No simple word,
40   That shall be utter'd at our mirthfull boord,
    Shall make us sad next morning: or affright
        The libertie, that wee'll enjoy to night.

[E-102]   TO WILLIAM EARLE OF PEMBROKE.

    I doe but name thee PEMBROKE, and I find
        It is an *Epigramme,* on all man-kind;
    Against the bad, but of, and to the good:
        Both which are ask'd,° to have thee understood.   *evoked*
5   Nor could the age have mist° thee, in this strife   *missed*
        Of vice, and vertue; wherein all great life
    Almost, is exercis'd: and scarce one knowes,
        To which, yet, of the sides himselfe he owes.
    They follow vertue, for reward, to day;
10   To morrow vice, if shee give better pay:
    And are so good, and bad, just at a price,
        As nothing else discernes the vertue'or vice.
    But thou, whose noblêsse keeps one stature still,
        And one true posture, though besieg'd with ill
15   Of what ambition, faction, pride can raise;
        Whose life, ev'n they, that envie it, must praise;
    That art so reverenc'd, as° thy comming in,   *that*
        But in the view, doth interrupt their sinne;
    Thou must draw more:° and they, that hope to see   *to your party*
20   The common-wealth still° safe, must studie thee.   *as yet, always*

---

beere: German beer, not highly esteemed by Jonson
36 **Pooly ... Parrot**: government spies in the 1590s; Jonson also is punning on the indiscriminate chatter of a "Polly" parrot
37 **cups ... men**: we need not fear that anything indiscreet we say while drinking will be reported against us later to our detriment
E-102.title **WILLIAM ... PEMBROKE**: see the notes to the epistle dedicatory of *Epigrammes*
13 **keeps ... still**: always remains the same
14 **besieg'd ... ill**: perhaps a reference to the court party led by the earl of Northampton, who became an enemy to both Pembroke and Jonson

[E-104]   TO SUSAN COUNTESSE OF MONTGOMERY.

    Were they that nam'd you, prophets? Did they see,
        Even in the dew of grace, what you would bee?
    Or did our times require it, to behold
        A new SUSANNA, equall to that old?
5   Or, because some scarce thinke that storie true,
        To make those faithfull, did the *Fates* send you?
    And to your *Scene* lent no lesse dignitie
        Of birth, of match, of forme, of chastitie?
    Or, more then° borne for the comparison   *than*
10   Of former age, or glorie of our one,°   *own*
    Were you advanced, past those times, to be
        The light, and marke unto posteritie?
    Judge they, that can: Here I have rais'd to show
        A picture, which the world for yours must know,
15 And like it too; if they looke equally:°   *without prejudice*
        If not, 'tis fit for you, some should envy.

[E-105]   TO MARY LADY WROTH.

    MADAME, had all antiquitie beene lost,
        All historie seal'd up, and fables crost;°   *crossed out, obliterated*
    That we had left us, nor° by time, nor place,   *neither*
        Least mention of a *Nymph*, a *Muse*, a *Grace*,
5   But even their names were to be made a-new,
        Who could not but create them all, from you?
    He, that but saw you weare the wheaten hat,
        Would call you more then° CERES, if not that: *than*
    And, drest in shepheards tyre,° who would not say: *attire*
10   You were the bright OENONE, FLORA, or *May*?
    If dancing, all would cry th'*Idalian* Queene,
        Were leading forth the *Graces* on the greene:

E-104.title SUSAN ... MONTGOMERY: Susan de Vere (1587–1629), daughter of the earl of Oxford and wife of Philip Herbert, earl of Montgomery
4 SUSANNA: a virtuous woman wrongly accused of vice, whose story is told in the book of Susanna in the Apocrypha
E-105.title MARY ... WROTH: Mary Sidney (1561–1621), daughter of Robert, first earl of Leicester, and niece of Sir Philip Sidney, wife of Sir Robert Wroth (or Worth), who proved to be a "Jealous husband" (*Conversations* 355–56), and herself a poet; Jonson addressed three poems and dedicated *The Alchemist* to her and wrote one poem to her husband (F-3)
7 wheaten hat: traditionally worn by **CERES (8)**, the Roman goddess of the grain harvest
10 OENONE: a beautiful nymph courted by the Trojan prince Paris, who subsequently deserted her for Helen; **FLORA**: the Roman goddess of flowers; *May*: the queen of the Mayday celebration
11 th'*Idalian* Queene: Aphrodite (or Venus), goddess of love and beauty
12 *Graces*: three Greek goddesses who represented beauty and charm

      And, armed to the chase, so bare her bow
         DIANA'alone, so hit, and hunted so.
15 There's none so dull, that for your stile° would aske,   *form of address*
         That saw you put on PALLAS plumed caske:°   *helmet*
      Or, keeping your due state,° that would not cry,   *social status*
         There JUNO sate, and yet no Peacock by.°   *near*
      So are you *Natures Index,*° and restore,   *summary*
20   I'your° selfe, all treasure lost of th'age before.   *in your*

[E-109]   TO SIR HENRY NEVIL.

Who now calls on thee, NEVIL, is a *Muse,*
    That serves nor° fame, nor titles; but doth chuse   *neither*
Where vertue makes them both, and that's in thee:
    Where all is faire, beside° thy pedigree.   *in addition to*
5 Thou art not one, seek'st miseries with hope,
    Wrestlest with dignities, or fain'st° a scope   *feigns*
Of service to the publique, when the end
    Is private gaine, which hath long guilt to friend.
Thou rather striv'st the matter to possesse,
10   And elements of honor, then° the dresse;°   *than/appearance*
To make thy lent life, good against the *Fates:*
    And first to know thine owne state, then the States.°   *State's state*
To be the same in roote, thou art in height;
    And that thy soule should give thy flesh her weight.
15 Goe on, and doubt not, what posteritie,
    Now I have sung thee thus, shall judge of thee.
Thy deedes, unto thy name, will prove new wombes,
    Whil'st others toyle for titles to their tombes.

[E-116]   TO SIR WILLIAM JEPHSON.

JEPHSON, thou man of men, to whose lov'd name
    All gentrie, yet, owe part of their best flame!
So did thy vertue'enforme, thy wit sustaine

---

14 **DIANA**: chaste Roman goddess of the hunt
16 **PALLAS**: Athene, Greek goddess of wisdom
18 **JUNO**: queen of the Roman gods, known for her majesty and dignity; the **Peacock** is sacred to her
E-109.title **SIR . . . NEVIL**: courtier and politician (1564?–1615), implicated in the Essex plot of 1601, imprisoned and fined; released in 1603; he was a leading candidate for the secretaryship of State in 1612, but he failed to get the post
13 **To . . . height**: trees such as the oak were thought to put down roots to a depth that equaled their height above ground
E-116.title **SIR . . . JEPHSON**: a friend of Jonson's; knighted in 1603

That age, when thou stood'st up the master-braine:
5 Thou wert the first, mad'st merit know her strength,
   And those that lack'd it, to suspect at length,
'Twas not entayl'd on° title. That some word   *dependent upon*
   Might be found out as good, and not *my Lord*.
That *Nature* no such difference had imprest
10   In men, but every bravest was the best:
That bloud not mindes, but mindes did bloud adorne:
   And to live great, was better, then° great borne.   *than*
These were thy knowing arts: which who doth now
   Vertuously practise must at least allow
15 Them in, if not, from thee; or must commit
   A desperate solœcisme° in truth and wit.   *incongruity, mistake*

[E-120]   EPITAPH ON S.P. A CHILD OF Q.EL. CHAPPEL.

Weepe with me all you that read
      This little storie:
And know, for whom a teare you shed,
      Death's selfe is sorry.
5 'Twas a child, that so did thrive
      In grace, and feature,
As *Heaven* and *Nature* seem'd to strive
      Which own'd the creature.
Yeeres he numbred scarse thirteene
10   When *Fates* turn'd cruell,
Yet three fill'd *Zodiackes*° had he beene   *three years*
      The stages jewell;
And did act (what now we mone)
      Old men so duely,
15 As, sooth, the *Parcæ*° thought him one,   *Fates*
      He plai'd so truely.
So, by error, to his fate
      They all consented;
But viewing him since (alas, too late)
20   They have repented.
And have sought (to give new birth)
      In bathes to steepe him;
But, being so much too good for earth,
      Heaven vowes to keepe him.

E-120.title S.P. ... CHAPPEL: Salomon Pavy, one of the Children of Queen Elizabeth's Chapel, assigned to her Revels, an acting company; Pavy joined the company in 1600, played in Jonson's *Cynthia's Revels* (1600) and *Poetaster* (1601), and died in 1602 at the age of **scarse thirteene (9)**.

[E-124]   EPITAPH ON ELIZABETH, L.H.

    Would'st thou heare, what man can say
        In a little? Reader, stay.
    Under-neath this stone doth lye
        As much beautie, as could dye:
5   Which in life did harbour give
        To more vertue, then° doth live.   *than*
    If, at all, shee had a fault,
        Leave it buryed in this vault.
    One name was ELIZABETH,
10 Th'other let it sleepe with death:
    Fitter, where it dyed, to tell,
        Then° that it liv'd at all. Farewell.   *than*

[E-126]   TO HIS LADY, THEN M^(RS.) CARY.

    Retyr'd, with purpose your faire worth to praise,
        'Mongst *Hampton* shades, and PHŒBUS grove of bayes,°   *laurels*
    I pluck'd a branch; the jealous god did frowne,
        And bad° me lay th'usurped laurell downe: *bade*
5   Said I wrong'd him, and (which was more) his love.
        I answer'd, DAPHNE now no paine can prove.°   *experience, suffer*
    PHŒBUS replyed. Bold head, it is not shee:
        CARY my love is, DAPHNE but my tree.

[E-128]   TO WILLIAM ROE.

    ROE (and my joy to name) th'art now, to goe
        Countries, and climes, manners, and men to know,
    T'extract, and choose the best of all these knowne,
        And those to turne to bloud, and make thine owne:

E-124.title ELIZABETH, L.H.: several candidates have been proposed as the subject of this epitaph, but Jonson deliberately obscured her identity (see lines 10–12)
E-126.title M^(rs.) CARY: daughter of Sir Edward Carey; M^(rs.) (Mistress) is the Renaissance equivalent of Miss, indicating that she was not married
2 *Hampton*: Hampton Court, a royal palace near London; the laurel is sacred to the god PHŒBUS Apollo
6 DAPHNE: a nymph pursued by Apollo; to escape his pursuit, she was changed into a laurel, which became a symbol of poetic achievement
E-128.title WILLIAM ROE: brother (1585–1667) of Jonson's close friend Sir John Roe; Jonson addressed two epigrams to William
2 Countries . . . know: echoes the description of a voyage to "The cities of a world of nations, / With all their manners, mindes, and fashions" in Homer's *Odyssey* (1.506, George Chapman's translation)

5   May windes as soft as breath of kissing friends,
       Attend thee hence; and there, may all thy ends,
   As the beginnings here, prove purely sweet,
       And perfect in a circle alwayes meet.
   So, when we, blest with thy returne, shall see
10   Thy selfe, with thy first thoughts, brought home by thee,
   We each to other may this voyce enspire;
       This is that good ÆNEAS, past° through fire,   *passed*
   Through seas, stormes, tempests: and imbarqu'd for hell,
       Came backe untouch'd. This man hath travail'd well.

---

12 ÆNEAS: the pious Trojan hero whose arduous travels, including a journey to the underworld, are chronicled in Virgil's *Aeneid*
14 travail'd: the common Renaissance spelling for both "traveled" and "travailed" (toiled, suffered); Jonson is here playing on both meanings

The Forrest.

[F-1]   Why I write not of Love.

      Some act of *Love's* bound to reherse,
      I thought to binde him, in my verse:
      Which when he felt, Away (quoth hee)
      Can Poets hope to fetter mee?
5   It is enough, they once did get
      MARS, and my *Mother,* in their net:
      I weare not these my wings in vaine.
      With which he fled me: and againe,
      Into my ri'mes could ne're be got
10   By any arte. Then wonder not,
      That since, my numbers° are so cold,   *verses*
      When *Love* is fled, and I grow old.

[F-2]   To Penshurst.

      Thou art not, PENSHURST, built to envious show,
        Of touch, or marble; nor canst boast a row
      Of polish'd pillars, or a roofe of gold:
        Thou hast no lantherne, whereof tales are told;
5   Or stayre, or courts; but stand'st an ancient pile,°   *structure*
        And these grudg'd at, art reverenc'd the while.
      Thou joy'st in better markes,° of soyle, of ayre,   *remarkable features*
        Of wood, of water: therein thou art faire.
      Thou hast thy walkes for health, as well as sport:

F-1.1 Some ... reherse: required to relate some act of the god Love (Cupid)
6 MARS ... net Love's mother (Venus) and the war god Mars (her illicit lover) were surprised and captured in a golden net by her husband Vulcan
F-2.title PENSHURST: the country home of the Sidney family in Kent, then occupied by Sir Philip Sidney's brother Robert (1563–1626) and his family
1 envious show: throughout, Jonson contrasts the ancient, relatively modest Penshurst to the newer, grander prodigy houses built by the newly rich and powerful
2 touch: touchstone; fine black marble or basalt
4 lantherne: windowed room or cupola at the top of a great house, built only for outward show, not for use
6 grudg'd: begrudged, envied (by their neighbors)

10   Thy *Mount,* to which the *Dryads*° doe resort,   *wood nymphs*
        Where PAN, and BACCHUS their high feasts have made,
            Beneath the broad beech, and the chest-nut shade;
        That taller tree, which of a nut was set,
            At his great birth, where all the *Muses* met,
15   There, in the writhed barke, are cut the names
            Of many a SYLVANE, taken with his flames.
        And thence, the ruddy *Satyres* oft provoke
            The lighter *Faunes,* to reach thy *Ladies oke.*
        Thy copp's, too, nam'd of GAMAGE, thou hast there,
20   That never failes to serve thee season'd° deere,   *mature*
        When thou would'st feast, or exercise thy friends.
            The lower land, that to the river bends,
        Thy sheepe, thy bullocks, kine,° and calves doe feed: *cows*
            The middle grounds thy mares, and horses breed.
25   Each banke doth yeeld thee coneyes;° and the topps   *rabbits*
            Fertile of wood, ASHORE, and SYDNEY'S copp's,
        To crowne thy open table, doth provide
            The purpled pheasant, with the speckled side:
        The painted partrich lyes in every field,
30   And, for thy messe,° is willing to be kill'd.   *meal*
        And if the high swolne *Medway* faile thy dish,
            Thou hast thy ponds, that pay thee tribute fish,
        Fat, aged carps, that runne into thy net.
            And pikes, now weary their owne kinde to eat,
35   As loth, the second draught, or cast to stay,
            Officiously,° at first, themselves betray.   *eagerly, dutifully*
        Bright eeles, that emulate them, and leape on land,
            Before the fisher, or into his hand.
        Then hath thy orchard fruit, thy garden flowers,
40   Fresh as the ayre, and new as are the houres.
        The earely cherry, with the later plum,
            Fig, grape, and quince, each in his time doth come:

---

10 *Mount*: a small hill on the estate
11 **PAN**: mythical creature, half man half goat, a companion to **BACCHUS**, the Roman god of wine and revelry
13–14 **That . . . birth**: an oak planted on the estate to commemorate the birth of Sir Philip Sidney, 30 November 1554
16 **SYLVANE . . . flames**: country lover inspired by Sidney's love poetry; Sylvane is the Roman god of forests, fields, and herding
17–18 *Satyres* . . . *Faunes*: mythical woodland creatures
18 **Ladies oke**: according to tradition, a member of the family, Lady Leicester, went into labor under a tree on the estate, thereafter called "My Lady's Oak"
19 **copp's . . . GAMAGE**: a small grove of trees (coppice) near the entrance to the estate, named for Sir Robert's wife, Barbara Gamage
26 **ASHORE . . . copp's**: two small groves of trees on the estate
31 *Medway*: a river bordering the estate
35 **loth . . . stay**: reluctant to await the second drawing or casting of the net

>   The blushing apricot, and woolly peach
>   Hang on thy walls, that every child may reach.
> 45 And though thy walls be of the countrey stone,
>   They' are rear'd with no mans ruine, no mans grone,
>   There's none, that dwell about them, wish them downe;
>   But all come in, the farmer, and the clowne:°   *rustic*
>   And no one empty-handed, to salute
> 50   Thy lord, and lady, though they have no sute.°   *suit: request, petition*
>   Some bring a capon, some a rurall cake,
>   Some nuts, some apples; some that thinke they make
>   The better cheeses, bring 'hem; or else send
>   By their ripe daughters, whom they would commend
> 55 This way to husbands; and whose baskets beare
>   An embleme° of themselves, in plum, or peare.   *allegorical picture*
>   But what can this (more then° expresse their love)   *than*
>   Adde to thy free provisions, farre above
>   The neede of such? whose liberall boord doth flow,
> 60   With all, that hospitalitie doth know!
>   Where comes no guest, but is allow'd to eate,
>   Without his feare, and of thy lords owne meate:
>   Where the same beere, and bread, and selfe-same wine,
>   That is his Lordships, shall be also mine.
> 65 And I not faine° to sit (as some, this day,   *disposed*
>   At great mens tables) and yet dine away.
>   Here no man tells my cups;° nor, standing by,   *counts my drinks*
>   A waiter, doth my gluttony envy:
>   But gives me what I call,° and lets me eate,   *call for*
> 70   He knowes, below, he shall finde plentie of meate,
>   Thy tables hoord not up for the next day,
>   Nor, when I take my lodging, need I pray°   *have to ask*
>   For fire, or lights, or livorie:° all is there;   *provisions*
>   As if thou, then, wert mine, or I raign'd here:
> 75 There's nothing I can wish, for which I stay.°   *must wait*
>   That found King JAMES, when hunting late, this way,
>   With his brave sonne, the Prince, they saw thy fires
>   Shine bright on every harth as° the desires   *as if*
>   Of thy *Penates* had beene set on flame,

---

44 Hang ... walls: are trained to grow flat (espaliered) against the garden walls
66 away: in a different place; that is, be forced to dine elsewhere because here they are served less and worse food than that provided to the great men present at the same table; in just such a situation, Jonson protested to Robert Cecil, earl of Salisbury, owner of the lavish country estate Theobalds, "My Lord ... yow promised I should dine with yow, bot I doe not" since he had none of the food served to Salisbury himself (*Conversations* 318–19)
68 waiter ... envy: at some great houses, the servants were fed only the leftover scraps after everyone else had eaten; hence they would begrudge those guests who ate and drank to excess
77 Prince: Henry, elder son of James I; he died 6 November 1612 at the age of eighteen
79 Penates: the household gods of ancient Rome, here standing for the gods of hospitality

25

80	To entertayne them; or the countrey came,	
	With all their zeale, to warme their welcome here.	
	What (great, I will not say, but) sodayne° cheare	*sudden*
	Did'st thou, then, make 'hem! and what praise was heap'd	
	On thy good lady, then! who, therein, reap'd	
85	The just reward of her high huswifery;	
	To have her linnen, plate,° and all things nigh,	*gold or silver dishes*
	When shee was farre: and not a roome, but drest,	
	As if it had expected such a guest!	
	These, PENSHURST, are thy praise, and yet not all.	
90	Thy lady's noble, fruitfull, chaste withall.°	*in addition*
	His children thy great lord may call his owne:	
	A fortune, in this age, but rarely knowne.	
	They are, and have beene taught religion: Thence	
	Their gentler spirits have suck'd innocence.	
95	Each morne, and even, they are taught to pray,	
	With the whole houshold, and may, every day,	
	Reade, in their vertuous parents noble parts,	
	The mysteries of manners, armes, and arts.	
	Now, PENSHURST, they that will proportion° thee	*compare*
100	With other edifices, when they see	
	Those proud, ambitious heaps, and nothing else,	
	May say, their lords have built, but thy lord dwells.	

[F-3]   TO SIR ROBERT WROTH.

	How blest art thou, canst love the countrey, WROTH,	
	Whether by choice, or fate, or both;	
	And, though so neere the citie, and the court,	
	Art tane° with neithers vice, nor sport:	*taken*
5	That at great times, art no ambitious guest	
	Of Sheriffes dinner, or Maiors° feast.	*Mayor's*
	Nor com'st to view the better cloth of state;	
	The richer hangings, or crowne-plate;°	*royal dishes of silver or gold*
	Nor throng'st (when masquing is) to have a sight	
10	Of the short braverie° of the night;	*ephemeral splendor*
	To view the jewells, stuffes,° the paines, the wit	*clothing*
	There wasted, some not paid for yet!	
	But canst, at home, in thy securer° rest,	*freer from worry*

---

98 **mysteries**: crafts, arts, but with a sense of the mysteries of a religion, into which one must be initiated
F-3.title **SIR . . . WROTH**: husband (1576–1614) of Jonson's friend Lady Mary (see notes to E-105), who enters the poem at line 55; son-in-law of Sir Robert Sidney; knighted in 1601
3 **neere . . . citie**: Sir Robert's estate, Durrants, was a few miles northeast of London
9 **masquing**: the performance of court masques

26

  Live, with un-bought provision blest;
15 Free from proud porches, or their guilded roofes,
   'Mongst loughing heards,° and solide hoofes: *lowing herds*
  Along'st the curled woods, and painted meades,° *flowering meadows*
   Through which a serpent river leades
  To some coole, courteous shade, which he calls his,
20 And makes sleepe softer then° it is!   *than*
  Or, if thou list° the night in watch to breake,   *wish*
   A-bed canst heare the loud stag speake,
  In spring, oft roused for thy masters sport,
   Who, for it, makes thy house his court;
25 Or with thy friends, the heart of all the yeere,°   *the summer*
   Divid'st, upon the lesser Deere;
  In autumne, at the Partrich makes a flight,
   And giv'st thy gladder guests the sight;
  And, in the winter, hunt'st the flying hare,
30 More for thy exercise, then° fare;   *than*
  While all, that follow, their glad eares apply
   To the full greatnesse of the cry:°   *baying of the hounds*
  Or hauking at the river, or the bush,
   Or shooting at the greedie thrush,
35 Thou dost with some delight the day out-weare,
   Although the coldest of the yeere!
  The whil'st, the severall seasons thou hast seene
   Of flowrie fields, of cop'ces° greene,   *coppices: thickets*
  The mowed meddowes, with the fleeced sheepe,
40 And feasts, that either shearers keepe;
  The ripened eares, yet humble in their height,
   And furrowes laden with their weight;
  The apple-harvest, that doth longer last;
   The hogs return'd home fat from mast;° *the nuts of forest trees*
45 The trees cut out in log; and those boughes made
   A fire now, that lent a shade!
  Thus PAN, and SYLVANE, having had their rites,
   COMUS puts in, for new delights,
  And fills thy open hall with mirth, and cheere,
50 As if in SATURNES raigne it were;
  APOLLO'S harpe, and HERMES lyre resound,
   Nor are the *Muses* strangers found:

---

23 thy masters: the king's; the greatest stags were reserved for the king's hunting; others could hunt only the **lesser Deere (26)**
40 either shearers: either those of the meadows (the mowers) or those of the sheep
47–52 PAN: mythical creature, half man half goat; **SYLVANE**: Roman god of forests, fields, and herding; **COMUS**: god of mirth and revelry; **SATURNES raigne**: the Golden Age; **APOLLO'S . . . lyre**: the origins of these instruments are attributed to these two Greek gods; **Muses**: patronesses of the arts

The rout of rurall folke come thronging in,
   (Their rudenesse° then is thought no sinne)   *rustic lack of manners*
55 Thy noblest spouse affords them welcome grace;
   And the great *Heroes,* of her race,
Sit mixt with losse of state,° or reverence.   *with no regard to status*
   Freedome doth with degree dispense.
The jolly wassall walkes the often round,°   *cups are frequently refilled*
60   And in their cups, their cares are drown'd:
They thinke not, then, which side the cause shall leese,°   *lose*
   Nor how to get the lawyer fees.
Such, and no other was that age, of old,
   Which boasts t'have had the head° of gold.   *heading, title*
65 And such since thou canst make thine owne content,
   Strive, WROTH, to live long innocent.
Let others watch in guiltie armes, and stand
   The furie of a rash command,
Goe enter breaches, meet the cannons rage,
70   That they may sleepe with scarres in age.
And shew their feathers shot, and cullors° torne,   *ensigns, flags*
   And brag, that they were therefore borne.
Let this man sweat, and wrangle at the barre,
   For every price, in every jarre,°   *disagreement*
75 And change possessions, oftner with his breath,
   Then° either money, warre, or death: *than*
Let him, then° hardest sires, more disinherit,   *than*
   And each where° boast it as his merit,   *in each instance*
To blow up orphanes, widdowes, and their states;°   *estates*
80   And thinke his power doth equall *Fates.*
Let that goe heape a masse of wretched wealth,
   Purchas'd° by rapine, worse then° stealth,   *acquired/than*
And brooding o're it sit, with broadest° eyes,   *wide open*
   Not doing good, scarce when he dyes.
85 Let thousands more goe flatter vice, and winne,
   By being organes° to great sinne,   *instruments*
Get place, and honor, and be glad to keepe
   The secrets, that shall breake° their sleepe: *interrupt*
And, so they ride in purple, eat in plate,°   *gold or silver dishes*
90   Though poyson, thinke it a great fate.
But thou, my WROTH, if I can truth apply,
   Shalt neither that, nor this envy:
Thy peace is made; and, when man's state is well,
   'Tis better, if he there can dwell.
95 God wisheth, none should wracke° on a strange shelfe:°   *wreck/sandbar*
   To him, man's dearer, then° t'himselfe.   *than*
And, howsoever we may thinke things sweet,
   He always gives what he knowes meet;°   *appropriate*
Which who can use is happy: Such be thou.

28

100   Thy morning's, and thy evening's vow
         Be° thankes to him, and earnest prayer, to finde   *should be*
      A body sound, with sounder minde;
         To doe thy countrey service, thy selfe right;
      That neither want doe thee affright,
105   Nor death; but when thy latest° sand is spent,   *last*
         Thou maist thinke life, a thing but lent.

[F-4]   TO THE WORLD.
           A farewell for a Gentle-woman, vertuous and noble.

      False world, good-night: since thou hast brought
         That houre upon my morne of age,
      Hence-forth I quit thee from my thought,
         My part is ended on thy stage.
5   Doe not once hope, that thou canst tempt
         A spirit so resolv'd to tread
      Upon thy throate, and live exempt
         From all the nets that thou canst spread.
      I know thy formes are studyed arts,
10   Thy subtle wayes, be narrow straits;
      Thy curtesie but sodaine° starts,   *sudden*
         And what thou call'st thy gifts are baits.
      I know too, though thou strut, and paint,°   *use cosmetics*
         Yet art thou both shrunke up, and old,
15   That onely fooles make thee a saint,
         And all thy good is to be sold.
      I know thou whole° art but a shop   *wholly, entirely*
         Of toyes, and trifles, traps, and snares,
      To take° the weake, or make them stop: *captivate*
20   Yet art thou falser then° thy wares.   *than*
      And, knowing this, should I yet stay,
         Like such as blow away their lives,
      And never will redeeme a day,
         Enamor'd of their golden gyves?°   *shackles, fetters*
25   Or, having scap'd, shall I returne,
         And thrust my necke into the noose,
      From whence, so lately, I did burne,
         With all my powers, my selfe to loose?
      What bird, or beast, is knowne so dull,
30   That fled his cage, or broke his chaine,
      And tasting ayre, and freedome, wull°   *will*
         Render° his head in there againe?   *restore*

F-4.title **Gentle-woman**: unidentified; she is the speaker of the poem

>   If these, who have but sense, can shun
>   The engines,° that have them annoy'd;°   *snares/troubled*
> 35   Little, for me, had reason done,
>   If I could not thy ginnes° avoyd.   *engines: snares*
>   Yes, threaten, doe. Alas I feare
>   As little, as I hope from thee:
>   I know thou canst nor° shew, nor beare   *neither*
> 40   More hatred, then° thou hast to mee.   *than*
>   My tender, first, and simple yeeres
>   Thou did'st abuse, and then betray;
>   Since stird'st up jealousies and feares,
>   When all the causes were away.°   *absent, nonexistent*
> 45   Then, in a soile° hast planted me,   *perhaps at court*
>   Where breathe the basest of thy fooles;
>   Where envious arts professed be,
>   And pride, and ignorance the schooles,
>   Where nothing is examin'd, weigh'd,
> 50   But, as 'tis rumor'd, so beleev'd:
>   Where every freedome is betray'd,
>   And every goodnesse tax'd, or griev'd.
>   But, what we' are borne for, we must beare:
>   Our fraile condition it is such,
> 55   That, what to all may happen here,
>   If't chance to me, I must not grutch.°   *murmur, complain*
>   Else, I my state should much mistake,
>   To harbour a divided thought°   *a thought that separates me*
>   From all my kinde: that, for my sake,
> 60   There should a miracle be wrought.
>   No, I doe know, that I was borne
>   To age, misfortune, sicknesse, griefe:
>   But I will beare these, with that scorne,
>   As shall not need thy false reliefe.
> 65   Nor for my peace will I goe farre,
>   As wandrers doe, that still° doe rome,   *always*
>   But make my strengths, such as they are,
>   Here in my bosome, and at home.

---

33 **but sense**: only sense impressions; that is, they lack reasoning powers

[F-5]   *Song.*
                    TO CELIA.

	Come my CELIA, let us prove,°	*attempt*
	While we may, the sports of love;	
	Time will not be ours, for ever:	
	He, at length, our good will sever.	
5	Spend not then his guifts in vaine.	
	Sunnes, that set, may rise againe:	
	But if once we loose° this light,	*lose*
	'Tis, with us, perpetuall night.	
	Why should we deferre our joyes?	
10	Fame,° and rumor are but toyes.	*reputation*
	Cannot we delude the eyes	
	Of a few poore houshold spyes?	
	Or his easier eares beguile,	
	So removed by our wile?	
15	'Tis no sinne, loves fruit to steale,	
	But the sweet theft to reveale:	
	To be taken,° to be seene,	*caught*
	These have crimes accounted beene.	

[F-6]   TO THE SAME.

	Kisse me, sweet: The warie lover	
	Can your favours keepe, and cover,	
	When the common courting jay	
	All your bounties will betray.	
5	Kisse againe: no creature comes.	
	Kisse, and score° up wealthy summes	*count*
	On my lips, thus hardly sundred,	
	While you breath.° First give a hundred,	*breathe*
	Then a thousand, then another	
10	Hundred, then unto the tother	
	Adde a thousand, and so more:	
	Till you equall with the store,	

F-5.title: Jonson included this song in *Volpone* 3.7.166–83 (1606), where the lascivious title character (whose name means "fox") sings it in an attempt to woo **CELIA** (or "heavenly"), the virtuous young wife of rapacious old Corvino (Crow); in that context, **his (13)** refers to Corvino; the poem is based on Catullus 4:3–6
F-6: Jonson included lines 19–22 in *Volpone* 3.7.236–39 (see note to F-5); the poem is based on Catullus 5.7–13 and 7

31

All the grasse that *Rumney* yeelds,
Or the sands in *Chelsey* fields,
15 Or the drops in silver *Thames,*
Or the starres, that guild° his streames,   *gild*
In the silent sommer-nights,
When youths ply their stolne delights.
That the curious may not know
20 How to tell'hem,° as thy flow,   *count them*
And the envious, when they find
What their number is, be pin'd.°   *pained, distressed*

[F-7]   *Song.*
        THAT WOMEN ARE BUT MENS SHADDOWES.

Follow a shaddow, it still° flies° you;   *always/flees from*
  Seeme to flye it, it will pursue:
So court a mistris, shee denyes you;
  Let her alone, shee will court you.
5 Say, are not women truely, then,
  Stil'd° but the shaddowes of us men?   *properly referred to as*
At morne, and even, shades are longest;
  At noone, they are or° short, or none: *either*
So men at weakest, they° are strongest,   *women*
10 But grant us perfect,° they're not knowne.   *upright, fully grown*
Say, are not women truely, then,
  Stil'd but the shaddowes of us men?

[F-8]   TO SICKNESSE.

Why, *Disease,* dost thou molest
Ladies? and of them the best?
Doe not men, ynow° of rites   *enough*
To thy altars, by their nights
5 Spent in surfets: and their dayes,
And nights too, in worser wayes?
  Take heed, *Sicknesse,* what you doe,

---

13 Rumney: Romney Marsh in Kent
14 Chelsey: Chelsea, a rural area in Jonson's time, now a part of Greater London; the name derives from "chesil" (gravel)
F-7: adapted from a Latin poem by Barthélemi Aneau; Jonson told Drummond of Hawthornden how this poem came to be written: "Pembroke and his Lady discoursing, the Earl said the Woemen were mens shadowes, and she maintained them [as independent beings], both appealing to Johnson, he affirmed it [Pembroke's position] true, for which my Lady gave a pennance to prove it in Verse, hence his Epigrame" (*Conversations* 364–67)

      I shall feare, you'll surfet too.
      Live not we, as, all thy stalls,°   *assigned places*
10   Spittles,° pest-house, hospitalls,   *hospitals for the poor*
      Scarce will take our present store?
          And this age will build no more:
          'Pray thee, feed contented, then,
          Sicknesse; onely on us men.
15   Or if needs thy lust will tast
          Woman-kinde; devoure the wast°   *waste, profligate*
          Livers, round about the towne.
      But, forgive me, with thy crowne°   *sovereignty, authority, also a coin*
      They maintayne the truest trade,
20   And have more diseases made.
          What should, yet, thy pallat please?
          Daintinesse, and softer ease,
          Sleeked limmes,° and finest blood?   *limbs*
          If thy leanenesse love such food,
25   There are those, that, for thy sake,
          Doe enough; and who would take
          Any paines; yea, thinke it price,°   *worthy, excellent*
          To become thy sacrifice.
          That distill° their husbands land   *dissolve, transform*
30   In decoctions;° and are mann'd   *acts of boiling down*
          With ten Emp'ricks,° in their chamber,   *experimenters*
          Lying for the spirit of amber.°   *acid distilled from amber*
          That for th'oyle of *Talke*,° dare spend   *oil of talc (a cosmetic)*
          More then° citizens dare lend   *than*
35   Them, and all their officers.
          That, to make all pleasure theirs,
          Will by coach, and water goe,
          Every stew° in towne to know;   *brothel*
          Dare entayle° their loves on any,   *bestow, confer*
40   Bald, or blinde, or nere so many:
          And, for thee, at common game,°   *gambling*
          Play away, health, wealth, and fame.°   *reputation*
      These, *disease*, will thee deserve:
      And will, long ere thou should'st starve
45   On their beds, most prostitute,
      Move it, as their humblest sute,°   *suit: plea, request*
      In thy justice to molest
      None but them, and leave the rest.

[F-9] *Song.*
         TO CELIA.

    Drinke to me, onely, with thine eyes,
        And I will pledge with mine;
    Or leave a kisse but in the cup,
        And Ile not looke for wine.
5   The thirst, that from the soule doth rise,
        Doth aske a drinke divine:
    But might I of JOVE'S *Nectar* sup,
        I would not change° for thine.   *exchange*
    I sent thee, late,° a rosie wreath,   *lately, recently*
10   Not so much honoring thee,
    As giving it a hope, that there
        It could not withered bee.
    But thou thereon did'st onely breath,°   *breathe*
        And sent'st it backe to mee:
15   Since when it growes, and smells, I sweare,
        Not of it selfe, but thee.

[F-10]

    And must I sing? what subject shall I chuse?
    Or whose great name in *Poets* heaven use?
    For the more countenance to° my active *Muse?*   *better repute of*

    HERCULES? alas his bones are yet sore,
5   With his old earthly labours. T'exact more,
    Of his dull god-head, were sinne. Ile implore

    PHŒBUS. No? tend thy cart° still.° Envious day   *chariot/as yet, always*
    Shall not give out,° that I have made thee stay,°   *report/stop*
    And foundred thy hot teame, to tune my lay.°   *song, poem*

10   Nor will I beg of thee, *Lord of the vine,*

F-9: see F-5 and F-6; this poem is based on five passages in the prose *Epistles* of the Greek rhetorician Philostratus (170–ca. 245), written to a boy with whom he was infatuated

F-10: an untitled prefatory poem to F-11; both originally appeared, in slightly different texts, in an appendix to Robert Chester's poem *Loves Martyr* (1601), along with Shakespeare's "The Phoenix and the Turtle" and other poems on the same theme by John Marston and George Chapman; the phoenix is the Platonic ideal of the perfect woman and the turtledove is the perfect, faithful man

4–5 HERCULES ... labours: the twelve arduous labors of the mythical Greek hero Hercules, carried out on the orders of King Eurystheus; the best known account is in Ovid's *Metamorphoses* 9.182–98

7 PHŒBUS: the god Apollo, who carries the sun across the sky each day in a **cart**

10 Lord ... vine: the god Dionysus (or Bacchus), who is most often pictured wearing a

To raise my spirits with thy conjuring wine,
In the greene circle of thy Ivy twine.

PALLAS, nor thee I call on, mankinde° maid,   *masculine*
That, at thy birth, mad'st the poore Smith affraid,
15 Who, with his axe, thy fathers mid-wife plaid.

Goe, crampe° dull MARS, light VENUS, when he snorts,°   *pinch/snores*
Or with thy *Tribade* trine, invent new sports,
Thou, nor thy loosenesse with my making° sorts.°   *composing/is suitable*

Let the *old boy,* your sonne, ply his old taske,
20 Turne the stale prologue to some painted maske,
His absence in my verse, is all I aske.

HERMES, the cheater, shall not mixe with us,
Though he would steale his sisters PAGASUS,
And riffle° him: or pawne his PETASUS.   *raffle, gamble away*

25 Nor all the ladies of the *Thespian lake,*
(Though they were crusht into one forme) could make
A beautie of that merit, that should take

My *Muse* up by *commission:*° No, I bring   *order, command*
My owne true fire. Now my thought takes wing,
30 And now an *Epode* to deepe° eares I sing.   *profound, wise, serious*

---

greene circle of . . . Ivy (12) on his head
13 **PALLAS**: Pallas Athene, goddess of wisdom and defensive war, who was born, full grown and in armor, from the head of her father Zeus when it was struck with an **axe (15)** by the **Smith (14)** god Hephaestus (or Vulcan)
16 **MARS**: god of war; **VENUS**, goddess of illicit love, therefore **light**; the two were caught sleeping together after an adulterous union by her husband Vulcan; she was subsequently comforted by the three Graces, called here **thy *Tribade* trine (17)**, that is, three lesbians
19 ***old boy***: Cupid, an ancient god, but always remaining a child
22 **HERMES . . . cheater**: Hermes (or Mercury) was the god of thieves and merchants
23 **PAGASUS**: Pegasus, the winged horse, traditionally the symbol of inspiration; striking the ground with his hoof, he created the sacred Hippocrene spring for Hermes's **sisters**, the Muses
24 **PETASUS**: the winged hat of Hermes
25 **ladies . . . lake**: the Muses, whose fountain Aganippe is at the foot of Mt. Helicon, near Thespia
30 ***Epode***: see the note to the title of F-11

[F-11]   EPODE.

     Not to know vice at all, and keepe true state,°   *manner of living*
         Is vertue, and not *Fate:*
     Next, to that vertue, is to know vice well,
         And her blacke spight° expell.   *spite*
5   Which to effect (since no brest is so sure,
         Or safe, but shee'll procure
     Some way of entrance) we must plant a guard
         Of thoughts to watch, and ward°   *protect, defend*
     At th'eye and eare (the ports° unto the minde)   *portals, doors*
10   That no strange, or unkinde°   *unnatural*
     Object arrive there, but the heart (our spie)
         Give knowledge instantly,
     To wakefull reason, our affections king:
         Who (in th'examining)
15 Will quickly taste° the treason, and commit°   *sense, recognize/commit to*
         Close,° the close° cause of it.   *strict control/immediate*
     Tis the securest policie we have,
         To make our sense our slave.
     But this true course is not embrac'd by many:
20   By many? scarse by any.
     For either our affections doe rebell,
         Or else the sentinell
     (That should ring larum° to the heart) doth sleepe,   *alarm*
         Or some great° thought doth keepe   *powerful, dominant*
25 Backe the intelligence, and falsely sweares,
         Th'are base, and idle feares
     Whereof the loyall conscience so complaines.
         Thus, by these subtle traines,°   *treacheries, deceits*
     Doe severall passions invade the minde,
30   And strike our reason blinde.
     Of which usurping rancke, some have thought love
         The first; as prone to move
     Most frequent tumults, horrors, and unrests,
         In our enflamed brests:
35 But this doth from the cloud of error grow,
         Which thus we over-blow.°   *blow away*
     The thing, they here call Love, is blinde Desire,
         Arm'd with bow, shafts, and fire;
     Inconstant, like the sea, of whence 'tis borne,
40   Rough, swelling, like a storme:

F-11.title EPODE: a poetic form invented by the Greek poet Archilochus (ca. 714–ca. 676 BC), written in couplets consisting of one long and one short line and either serious or satiric in approach; Jonson helped introduce the epode into English

With whom who sailes, rides on the surge of feare,
    And boyles,° as if he were   *boiling liquids*
In a continuall tempest. Now, true Love
    No such effects doth prove;°   *bring about, produce*
45 That is an essence, farre more gentle, fine,
    Pure, perfect, nay divine;
It is a golden chaine let downe from heaven,
    Whose linkes are bright, and even.
That falls like sleepe on lovers, and combines
50   The soft, and sweetest mindes
In equall knots: This beares no brands,° nor darts,   *swords*
    To murther different° hearts,   *separate, individual*
But, in a calme, and god-like unitie,
    Preserves communitie.
55 O, who is he, that (in this peace) enjoyes
    Th'*Elixir*° of all joyes?   *essence*
A forme more fresh, then° are the *Eden* bowers   *than*
    And lasting, as her flowers:
Richer then° *Time,* and as *Time's* vertue, rare.   *than*
60   Sober, as saddest° care: *most enduring, most steadfast*
A fixed thought, an eye un-taught to glance;
    Who (blest with such high chance)
Would, at suggestion of a steepe° desire,   *precipitous, headlong*
    Cast himselfe from the spire
65 Of all his happinesse? But soft: I heare
    Some vicious foole draw neare,
That cryes, we dreame, and sweares, there's no such thing,
    As this chaste love we sing.
Peace° Luxurie,° thou art like one of those   *be quiet/lust*
70   Who, being at sea, suppose,
Because they move, the continent doth so:
    No, vice, we let thee know
Though thy wild thoughts with sparrowes wings doe flye,
    Turtles° can chastly dye;   *turtledoves*
75 And yet (in this t'expresse our selves more cleare)
    We doe not number, here,

---

47 **golden ... heaven**: from Homer's *Iliad* 8.19; according to his note to *Hymenæi* 300, Jonson prefers the interpretation of this chain by the Latin grammarian Macrobius (fl. 400): "Mind" emanates from God and suffuses the whole of creation down to the lowest creature, binding all into an unbroken and unbreakable chain
58 **lasting ... flowers**: as eternal as Eden's flowers before the Fall introduced death into nature
59 ***Time's* vertue**: Truth, the daughter of Time
64 **Cast ... spire**: alluding to Satan's temptation of Christ on the pinnacle of the Temple (Matthew 4:5–6; Luke 4:9)
73 **sparrowes wings**: sparrows are symbolic of lechery
74 **dye**: with a pun on having sexual intercourse; see the first note to F-10

Such spirits as are onely continent,
        Because lust's meanes are spent:
Or those, who doubt the common mouth of fame,
80   And for their place, and name,°   *reputation*
Cannot so safely sinne. Their chastitie
        Is meere necessitie.
Nor meane we those, whom vowes and conscience
        Have fill'd with abstinence:
85 Though we acknowledge, who can so abstayne,
        Makes a most blessed gayne.
He that for love of goodnesse hateth ill,
        Is more crowne-worthy still,
Then° he, which for sinnes penaltie forbeares.   *than*
90   His heart sinnes, though he feares.
But we propose a person like our Dove,
        Grac'd with a Phœnix love;
A beautie of that cleere, and sparkling light,
        Would make a day of night,
95 And turne the blackest sorrowes to bright joyes:
        Whose od'rous breath destroyes
All taste of bitternesse, and makes the ayre
        As sweet, as shee is fayre.
A body so harmoniously compos'd,
100   As if *Nature* disclos'd
All her best symmetrie in that one feature!
        O, so divine a creature
Who could be false to? chiefly, when he knowes
        How onely shee bestowes
105 The wealthy° treasure of her love on him;   *superabundant, copious*
        Making his fortunes swim
In the full floud of her admir'd perfection?
        What savage, brute affection,
Would not be fearefull to offend a dame
110   Of this excelling frame?
Much more a noble, and right generous mind
        (To vertuous moods inclin'd)
That knowes the waight of guilt: He will refraine
        From thoughts of such a straine.
115 And to his sense object this sentence ever,
        Man may securely° sinne, but safely never.   *confidently*

---

79 **doubt ... fame:** fear scandal
92 **Phœnix:** see the first note to F-10
115 **to ... ever:** to his sensuality oppose this maxim always

[F-12]   *Epistle*
          TO ELIZABETH COUNTESSE OF RUTLAND.

   MADAME,
   Whil'st that, for which, all vertue now is sold,
      And almost every vice, almightie gold,
   That which, to boote° with hell, is thought worth heaven,   *be of value*
      And, for it, life, conscience, yea, soules are given,
5 Toyles, by grave° custome, up and downe the court,   *respected*
      To every squire, or groome, that will report
   Well, or ill, onely, all the following yeere,
      Just to the waight their this dayes-presents beare;
   While it makes huishers° serviceable men,   *ushers: servants*
10   And some one apteth° to be trusted, then,   *fittest*
   Though never after; whiles it gaynes the voyce
      Of some grand peere, whose ayre° doth make rejoyce   *manner*
   The foole that gave it; who will want, and weepe,
      When his proud patrons favours are asleepe;
15 While thus it buyes great grace, and hunts poore fame;
      Runs betweene man, and man; 'tweene dame, and dame;
   Solders crackt friendship; makes love last a day;
      Or perhaps lesse: whil'st gold beares all this sway,
   I, that have none (to send you) send you verse.
20   A present which (if elder° writs° reherse°   *older/writings/relate*
   The truth of times) was once of more esteeme,
      Then° this, our guilt,° nor golden age can deeme,   *than/gilded*
   When gold was made no weapon to cut throtes,
      Or put to flight ASTREA, when her° ingots   *gold's*
25 Were yet unfound,° and better plac'd in earth,   *uncast*
      Then,° here, to give pride fame, and peasants birth.°   *than/high birth*
   But let this drosse carry what price it will
      With noble ignorants, and let them still°   *as yet, always*
   Turne, upon scorned verse, their quarter-face:
30   With you, I know, my offring will find grace.
   For what a sinne 'gainst your great fathers spirit,
      Were it to thinke, that you should not inherit
   His love unto the *Muses*, when his skill
      Almost you have, or may have, when you will?
35 Wherein wise *Nature* you a dowrie gave,

F12.title ELIZABETH ... RUTLAND: see the note to E-79; Elizabeth married the Earl of Rutland in 1599; Jonson wrote this verse epistle as a gift for New Year's Day, 1600
8 Just ... waight: precisely proportionate
24 ASTREA: the goddess of Justice, who lived on earth during the Golden Age; when mankind became wicked, she returned to heaven as the constellation Virgo
29 quarter-face: almost completely averted face
31 great fathers: Sir Philip Sidney's

39

  Worth an estate, treble to that you have.
  Beautie, I know, is good, and bloud is more;
   Riches thought most: But, *Madame,* thinke what store
  The world hath seene, which all these had in trust,
40 And now lye lost in their forgotten dust.
  It is the *Muse,* alone, can raise to heaven,
   And, at her strong armes end, hold up, and even,°   *make equal*
  The soules, shee loves. Those other glorious° notes,   *boastful*
   Inscrib'd in touch° or marble, or the cotes°   *fine stone/coats of arms*
45 Painted, or carv'd upon our great-mens tombs,
   Or in their windowes; doe but prove the wombs,
  That bred them, graves: when they were borne, they di'd,°   *died*
   That had no *Muse* to make their fame abide.
  How many equall with the *Argive* Queene,°   *Helen of Troy*
50 Have beautie knowne, yet none so famous seene?
  ACHILLES was not first, that valiant was,
   Or, in an armies head, that, lockt in brasse,
  Gave killing strokes. There were brave men, before
   AJAX, or IDOMEN, or all the store,
55 That HOMER brought to *Troy;* yet none so live:
   Because they lack'd the sacred pen, could give
  Like life unto 'hem. Who heav'd HERCULES
   Unto the starres? or the *Tyndarides?*
  Who placed JASONS ARGO in the skie?
60 Or set bright ARIADNES crowne so high?
  Who made a lampe of BERENICES hayre?
   Or lifted CASSIOPEA in her chayre?
  But onely *Poets,* rapt° with rage° divine?   *ravished/inspiration*
   And such, or my hopes faile, shall make you shine.
65 You, and that other starre, that purest light,
   Of all LUCINA'S traine; LUCY the bright.
  Then° which, a nobler heaven it selfe knowes not.   *than*
   Who, though shee have a better verser got,
  (Or *Poet,* in the court account) then° I,   *than*
70 And, who doth me (though I not him) envy,
  Yet, for the timely favours shee hath done,
   To my lesse sanguine *Muse,* wherein she'hath wonne
  My gratefull soule, the subject of her powers,
   I have already us'd some happy houres,

51–54 ACHILLES ... AJAX ... IDOMEN: heroes of Homer's *Iliad*
57–62 HERCULES ... CASSIOPEA: legendary and mythological beings who ultimately were transformed into stars or constellations
66 LUCINA'S train: Queen Elizabeth's attendants; **LUCY**: the countess of Bedford (see the note to E-76); both "Lucina" and "Lucy" derive from the Latin "lux" (light, brightness)
68 better verser: perhaps Samuel Daniel, whom Jonson considered "no poet" (*Conversations* 24), or Michael Drayton

75   To her remembrance; which when time shall bring
       To curious light, to notes, I then shall sing,
   Will prove old ORPHEUS act no tale to be:
       For I shall move stocks, stones, no lesse then° he.   *than*
   Then all, that have but done my *Muse* least° grace,   *even the smallest*
80   Shall thronging come, and boast the happy place
   They hold in my strange° *poems*, which, as yet,   *unfamiliar, novel*
       Had not their forme touch'd by an English wit.
   There like a rich, and golden *pyramede*,°   *obelisk*
       Borne up by statues, shall I reare your head,
85   Above your under-carved ornaments,
       And show, how, to the life, my soule presents
   Your forme imprest there: not with tickling rimes,
       Or common places, filch'd, that take° these times,   *are applauded in*
   But high, and noble matter, such as flies
90   From brains entranc'd, and fill'd with extasies;
   Moodes, which the god-like SYDNEY oft did prove,
       And your brave friend, and mine so well did love.
   Who wheresoere he be . . . .
                      The rest is lost.

---

76 notes ... sing: according to *The Masque of Queens* 666-69, Jonson intended to write a poem celebrating British ladies; if he did so, it does not survive

77 ORPHEUS act: according to legend, trees and stones were moved to dance by the power of Orpheus's music

78 stocks: tree trunks, stumps; with a play on the figurative meaning, senseless or stupid persons

82 their ... wit: Jonson was the first to introduce many classical forms of poetry into English verse

92 your ... friend: her husband, the earl of Rutland

93 wheresoere ... be: Rutland was on one of his many travels when the poem was presented to the countess in 1600

94 The ... lost: the poem originally ended with a hope that Elizabeth would bear a son; by the time of the publication of *The Forrest* in 1616, the earl of Rutland was known to be impotent; the original ending, transcribed from Bodleian Library ms. Rawlinson 31, is as follows:

       Who where so ere he be, on what deare coast,
       Now thincking on you though to England lost
95   For that firme grace he holdes in your regard
       I that am gratefull for him have prepar'd,
       This hastie sacrifice wherein I reare
       A vow, as new and ominous as the yeare
       Before his swift and circled race be run
100   My best of wishes, may you beare a sonne.

Century years, in this case 1600, were though to be particularly **ominous (98)**, presaging events to come

[F-13]   *Epistle.*
             TO KATHERINE, LADY AUBIGNY:

    'Tis growne almost a danger to speake true
        Of any good minde, now: There are so few.
    The bad, by number, are so fortified,
        As what th'have lost t'expect, they dare deride.
5   So both the prais'd, and praisers suffer: Yet,
        For other's ill, ought none their good forget.
    I, therefore, who professe my selfe in love
        With every vertue, wheresoere it move,
    And howsoever; as I am at fewd
10 With sinne and vice, though with a throne endew'd;
    And, in this name, am given out° dangerous   *reputed to be*
        By arts, and practise of the vicious,
    Such as suspect them-selves, and thinke it fit
        For their owne cap'tall crimes, t'indite my wit;
15 I, that have suffer'd this; and, though forsooke
        Of *Fortune,* have not alter'd yet my looke,
    Or so my selfe abandon'd, as because
        Men are not just, or keepe no holy lawes
    Of nature, and societie, I should faint;
20 Or feare to draw true lines, 'cause others paint:
    I, *Madame,* am become your praiser. Where,
        If it may stand with your soft blush to heare,
    Your selfe but told unto your selfe, and see
        In my character, what your features bee,
25 You will not from the paper slightly° passe: *with indifference*
        No lady, but, at some time, loves her glasse.°   *mirror*
    And this shall be no false one, but as much
        Remov'd,° as you from need to have it such.   *distanced (from you)*
    Looke then, and see your selfe. I will not say
30 Your beautie; for you see that every day:
    And so doe many more. All which° can call   *of whom*
        It perfect, proper, pure, and naturall,
    Not taken up o'th'doctors, but as well
        As I, can say, and see it doth excell.
35 That° askes but to be censur'd° by the eyes: *your beauty/judged*

F-13.title KATHERINE ... AUBIGNY: daughter (died 1627) of Sir Gervase Clifton; in 1609, she married Esmé Stuart, Seigneur d'Aubigny, third duke of Lennox, Jonson's friend and patron, with whom the poet had lived from 1602 to 1607 and to whom he dedicated *Sejanus* (1605)
4 what ... t'expect: that is, goodness
24 character: detailed description; the ancient Greek form of the prose character, describing virtuous and vicious types of persons, had recently become popular among English writers
33 taken ... o'th'doctors: dependent on medical or cosmetic aids

42

And, in those outward formes, all fooles are wise.
Nor that your beautie wanted not a dower,°   *gift, marriage settlement*
   Doe I reflect. Some alderman has power,
Or cos'ning farmer of the customes so,
40   T'advance his doubtfull issue,° and ore-flow   *dubious ends*
   A Princes fortune: These are gifts of chance,
      And raise not vertue; they may vice enhance.
My mirror is more subtile, cleere, refin'd,
   And takes, and gives the beauties of the mind.
45 Though it reject not those of FORTUNE: such
   As bloud, and match.° Wherein, how more then° much   *marriage/than*
Are you engaged to your happy fate,
   For such a lot!° that mixt you with a state°   *fortune, destiny/condition*
Of so great title, birth, but vertue most,
50   Without which, all the rest were sounds,° or lost.   *empty words*
'Tis onely that° can time, and chance defeat: *virtue*
   For he, that once is good, is ever great.
Wherewith, then, *Madame,* can you better pay
   This blessing of your starres, then° by that way   *than*
55 Of vertue, which you tread? what if alone?
   Without companions? 'Tis safe to have none.
In single paths, dangers with ease are watch'd:
   Contagion in the prease° is soonest catch'd.   *press: crowd*
This makes, that wisely you decline° your life,   *turn aside*
60   Farre from the maze of custome, error, strife,
And keepe an even, and unalter'd gaite;
   Not looking by,° or backe (like those, that waite   *to the side*
Times, and occasions, to start forth, and seeme)°   *appear*
   Which though the turning world may dis-esteeme,
65 Because that studies spectacles, and showes,
   And after varyed, as fresh objects goes,
Giddie with change, and therefore cannot see
   Right, the right way: yet must your comfort bee
Your conscience, and not wonder, if none askes
70   For truthes complexion, where they all weare maskes.
Let who will follow fashions, and attyres,
   Maintayne their liedgers forth, for forraine wyres,
Melt downe their husbands land, to poure away
   On the close groome, and page, on new-yeeres day,
75 And almost, all dayes after, while they live;
   (They finde it both so wittie,° and safe to give.)   *clever*

---

39 cos'ning . . . customes: cheating tax collector
72 Maintayne . . . wyres: support their agents (leidgers) elsewhere to report (which way) foreign wires (are pulling fashions)
74 close . . . page: menservants (with the suggestion of illicit lovers)

43

Let 'hem on poulders, oyles, and paintings, spend,
    Till that no usurer, nor his bawds° dare lend   *agents*
Them, or their officers:° and no man know,   *deputies*
80   Whether it be a face they weare, or no.
Let 'hem waste body, and state;° and after all,   *estate*
    When their owne Parasites° laugh at their fall,   *hangers-on*
May they have nothing left, whereof they can
    Boast, but how oft they have gone wrong to man:
85 And call it their brave° sinne. For such there be   *fine*
    That doe sinne onely for the infamie:
And never thinke, how vice doth every houre,
    Eate on her clients, and some one devoure.
You, *Madame*, yong have learn'd to shunne these shelves,°   *sandbars*
90   Whereon the most of mankinde wracke° themselves,   *wreck*
And, keeping a just° course, have earely put   *true*
    Into your harbor, and all passage shut
Gainst stormes, or pyrats, that might charge° your peace;   *threaten*
    For which you worthy are the glad encrease
95 Of your blest wombe, made fruitfull from above,
    To pay your lord the pledges of chast love:
And raise a noble stemme, to give the fame,
    To CLIFTON'S bloud, that is deny'd their name.
Grow, grow, faire tree, and as thy branches shoote,
100 Heare, what the *Muses* sing about thy roote,
By me, their priest (if they can ought divine)
    Before the moones have fill'd their tripple trine,
To crowne the burthen which you goe withall,°   *therewith*
    It shall a ripe and timely issue fall,
105 T'expect the honors of great 'AUBIGNY:
    And greater rites, yet° writ in mysterie,   *as yet*
But which the *Fates* forbid me to reveale.
    Onely, thus much, out of a ravish'd° zeale,   *enraptured*
Unto your name, and goodnesse of your life,
110 They speake; since you are truely that rare wife,
Other great wives may blush at: when they see
    What your try'd manners are, what theirs should bee.
How you love one, and him you should; how still°   *always*
    You are depending on his word, and will;
115 Not fashion'd for the court, or strangers eyes;
    But to please him, who is the dearer prise
Unto himselfe, by being so deare to you.

---

77 **poulders**: powders; **paintings**: cosmetics
84 **gone . . . man**: indulged in carnal sins
98 **CLIFTON'S . . . name**: Lady Aubigny's father had no sons
102 **moones . . . trine**: nine months are completed

This makes, that your affections still° be new,	*always*
And that your soules conspire,° as° they were gone	*breathe together/as if*
120 Each into other, and had now made one.	
Live that one, still;° and as long yeeres doe passe,	*always*
Madame, be bold to use this truest glasse:°	*mirror*
Wherein, your forme, you still° the same shall finde!	*always*
Because nor° it can change, nor such a minde.	*neither*

[F-14]   *Ode.*
        TO SIR WILLIAM SYDNEY, ON HIS BIRTH-DAY.

Now that the harth is crown'd with smiling fire,	
And some doe drinke, and some doe dance.	
Some ring,	
Some sing,	
5 And all doe strive t'advance	
The gladnesse higher:	
Wherefore° should I	*why*
Stand silent by.	
Who not the least,	
10 Both love the cause, and authors of the feast?	
Give me my cup, but from the *Thespian* well,	
That I may tell to SYDNEY, what	
This day	
Doth say,	
15 And he may thinke on that	
Which I doe tell:	
When all the noyse	
Of these forc'd joyes,	
Are fled and gone,	
20 And he, with his best *Genius*° left alone.	*guardian spirit*
This day sayes, then, the number of glad yeeres	
Are justly summ'd, that make you man;	
Your vow	
Must now	
25 Strive all right wayes it can,	
T'out-strip your peeres:	
Since he doth lacke	
Of going backe	
Little, whose will	

F-14.title SIR ... SIDNEY: son (1590–1612) of Sir Robert Sidney (see notes to F-2); knighted in January 1611; the poem was written for his twenty-first birthday (see lines 21–22); some years earlier William had sparked a scandal by seriously wounding his schoolmaster
11 *Thespian* well: the well of the Muses

30   Doth urge him to runne wrong, or to stand still.
    Nor can a little of the common store,
        Of nobles vertue, shew in you;
            Your blood
            So good
35   And great, must seeke for new,
    And studie more:
        Not weary, rest
        On what's deceast.
            For they, that swell
40   With dust of ancestors, in graves but dwell.
    'Twill be exacted of your name, whose sonne,
        Whose nephew, whose grand-child you are;
            And men
            Will, then,
45 Say you have follow'd farre,
    When well begunne:
        Which must be now,
        They teach you, how.
            And he that stayes°   *pauses*
50   To live untill to morrow'hath lost two dayes.
    So may you live in honor, as in name,
        If with this truth you be inspir'd,
            So may
            This day
55 Be more, and long desir'd:
    And with the flame
        Of love be bright,
        As with the light
            Of bone-fires.° Then   *bonfires*
60   The Birth-day shines, when logs not burne, but men.

[F-15]   TO HEAVEN.

    Good, and great GOD, can I not thinke of thee,
        But it must, straight,° my melancholy bee?   *immediately*
    Is it interpreted in me disease,
        That, laden with my sinnes, I seeke for ease?
5   O, be thou witnesse, that the reynes dost know,
        And hearts of all, if I be sad for show,

---

42 **nephew ... grand-child**: William was the nephew of Sir Philip Sidney and grandson of Sir Henry Sidney, who was three times Queen Elizabeth's Lord Deputy of Ireland
F-15.5–6 **reynes ... hearts**: the reins (kidneys) were thought to be the seat of affections or feelings; Jonson is alluding here to Psalms 7:9: "for the righteous God trieth the hearts and reins"

And judge me after: if I dare pretend
   To ought but grace, or ayme at other end.
As thou art all, so be thou all to mee,
10   First, midst, and last, converted° one, and three;   *changed to both*
My faith, my hope, my love: and in this state,
   My judge, my witnesse, and my advocate.
Where have I beene this while exil'd from thee?
   And whither rap'd,° now thou but stoup'st to mee?   *enraptured*
15 Dwell, dwell here still:° O, being every-where,   *without moving, always*
   How can I doubt to finde thee ever, here?
I know my state, both full of shame, and scorne,
   Conceiv'd in sinne, and unto labour borne,
Standing with feare, and must with horror fall,
20   And destin'd unto judgement, after all.
I feele my griefes too, and there scarce is ground,
   Upon my flesh t'inflict another wound.
Yet dare I not complaine, or wish for death
   With holy PAUL, lest it be thought the breath
25 Of discontent; or that these prayers bee
   For wearinesse of life, not love of thee.

23–24 Yet ... PAUL: "O wretched man that I am! who shall deliver me from the body of this death?" (Romans 7:24)

Selections from
THE UNDER-WOOD.

[U-1]   *POEMS* OF DEVOTION.

[1.] The Sinners Sacrifice.
To the Holy Trinitie.

1. O holy, blessed, glorious *Trinitie*
Of persons, still° one God, in *Unitie*.   *always*
The faithfull mans beleeved Mysterie,
    Helpe, helpe to lift
5 2. My selfe up to thee, harrow'd, torne, and bruis'd
By sinne, and Sathan; and my flesh misus'd,
As my heart lies in peeces, all confus'd,
    O take my gift.
3. All-gracious God, the *Sinners sacrifice,*
10 A broken heart thou wert not wont° despise,   *accustomed to*
But 'bove the fat of rammes, or bulls, to prize
    An offring meet,°   *appropriate*
4. For thy acceptance. O, behold me right,
And take compassion on my grievous plight.
15 What odour° can be, then° a heart contrite,   *odor of burnt offerings/than*
    To thee more sweet?
5. *Eternall Father,* God, who did'st create
This All of nothing, gavest it forme, and fate,
And breath'st into it, life, and light, with state°   *a natural condition*
20   To worship thee.
6. *Eternall God the Sonne,* who not denyd'st
To take our nature; becam'st man, and dyd'st,
To pay our debts, upon thy Crosse, and cryd'st
    All's done in me.
25 7. *Eternall Spirit,* God from both proceeding,
Father and Sonne; the Comforter, in breeding

U-1.1.3 **Mysterie**: the concept of the Trinity is one of the "mysteries" of the Christianity to be accepted on faith alone
10 **A ... despise**: "a broken and a contrite heart, O God, thou wilt not despise" (Psalms 51:17)
11 **'bove ... bulls**: "And Samuel said, Hath the LORD as great delight in burnt-offerings and sacrifice, as in obeying the voice of the LORD? Behold, to obey is better than sacrifice and to hearken than the fat of rams" (1 Samuel 15:22)
24 **All's ... me**: alluding to the final words of Christ on the cross: "It is finished" (John 19:30)

>   Pure thoughts in man: with fiery zeale them feeding
>   For acts of grace.
>   8. Increase those acts, ô glorious *Trinitie*
> 30 Of persons, still° one God in *Unitie;*   *always*
>   Till I attaine the long'd-for mysterie
>   Of seeing your face.
>   9. Beholding one in three, and three in one,
>   A *Trinitie,* to shine in *Union;*
> 35 The gladdest light, darke man can thinke upon;
>   O grant it me!°   *to me*
>   10. Father, and Sonne, and Holy Ghost, you three
>   All coeternall in your Majestie,
>   Distinct in persons, yet in Unitie
> 40   One God to see.
>   11. My Maker, Saviour, and my Sanctifier,
>   To heare, to meditate, sweeten my desire,
>   With grace, with love, with cherishing intire,
>   O, then how blest;
> 45 12. Among thy Saints elected to abide,
>   And with thy Angels, placed side, by side,
>   But in thy presence, truly glorified
>   Shall I there rest?

[2.] A Hymne to God the Father.

>   Heare mee, O God!
>   A broken heart,
>   Is my best part:
>   Use still° thy rod,   *always*
> 5   That I may prove°   *know by experience*
>   Therein, thy Love.
>
>   If thou hadst not
>   Beene sterne to mee,
>   But left me free,
> 10 I had forgot
>   My selfe and thee.
>
>   For, sin's so sweet,
>   As° minds ill bent   *that*

---

32 seeing ... face: "For now we see through a glass, darkly; but then face to face" (1 Corinthians 13:12); "Beloved, now are we the sons of God, and it doth not yet appear what we shall be: but we know that, when he shall appear, we shall be like him; for we shall see him as he is" (1 John 3:2)
U-1.2.4–6 Use ... Love: "For whom the Lord loveth he chasteneth, and scourgeth every son whom he receiveth" (Hebrews 12:6)

        Rarely repent,
15 Untill they meet
        Their punishment.

   Who more can crave
       Then° thou hast done: *than*
   That gav'st a Sonne,
20 To free a slave?
    First made of nought;
    Withall since bought.°   *ransomed (from sin)*

   Sinne, Death, and Hell,
     His° glorious Name   *Christ's*
25   Quite overcame,
   Yet I rebell,
    And slight the same.

   But, I'le come in,
    Before my losse,
30   Me farther tosse,°   *cast (away from God)*
   As sure to win
    Under his Crosse.

[3.] A Hymne On the Nativitie of my Saviour.

   I sing the birth, was borne to night,
   The Author both of Life, and light;
       The Angels so did sound° it,   *speak of, sing of*
   And like° the ravish'd Sheep'erds said,   *the same*
5 Who saw the light, and were afraid,
       Yet search'd, and true they found it.

   The Sonne of God, th'Eternall King,
   That did us all salvation bring,
       And freed the soule from danger;
10 Hee whom the whole world could not take,°   *contain*
   The Word, which heaven, and earth did make;
       Was now laid in a Manger.

   The Fathers wisedome will'd it so,
   The Sonnes obedience knew no No,

---

22 **Withall**: nevertheless, with a play on "with all"
U-1.3.3-6 **The . . . it**: See Luke 2:8-17
11 **Word . . . make**: "In the beginning was the Word, and the Word was with God, and the Word was God . . . . All things were made by him" (John 1:1,3)

15   Both wills were in one stature;
And as that wisedome had decreed,
The Word was now made Flesh indeed,°   *with a play on "in deed"*
     And tooke on him our Nature.

What comfort by him doe wee winne?
20 Who made himselfe the price of sinne,
     To make us heires of glory?
To see this Babe, all innocence;
A Martyr borne in our defence;
     Can man forget this Storie?

[U-2]   A Celebration of CHARIS in ten Lyrick Peeces.

           1. *His Excuse for loving.*

Let it not your wonder move,
Lesse your laughter; that I love.
Though I now write fiftie yeares,
I have had, and have my Peeres;
5 Poëts, though devine are men:
Some have lov'd as old agen.°   *that is, at twice my age*
And it is not always face,
Clothes, or Fortune gives the grace;
Or the feature,° or the youth: *comeliness, handsomeness*
10 But the Language, and the Truth,
With the Ardor, and the Passion,
Gives the Lover weight, and fashion.
If you then will read the Storie,
First, prepare you to be sorie,
15 That you never knew till now,
Either whom to love, or how:
But be glad, as soone with me,
When you know, that this is she,
Of whose Beautie it was sung,
20 She shall make the old man young

---

15 **Both ... stature**: the will of the Father and the will of the Son were exactly the same
17 **Word ... Flesh**: "And the Word was made flesh, and dwelt among us" (John 1:14)
20 **price ... sinne**: "ye are bought with a price" (1 Corinthians 6:20, 7:23)
21 **heires ... glory**: "we are the children of God: And if children, then heirs; heirs of God, and joint-heirs with Christ; if so be that we suffer with him, that we may be also glorified together" (Romans 8:16–17); see also James 2:5
U-2.title **CHARIS**: from the Latin *caritas* (love); if she was an actual person, her identity is unknown; in this sequence Jonson parodies several forms and conventions of Renaissance love poetry

    Keepe the middle age at stay,°   *at a stop, without forward movement*
    And let nothing high decay.
    Till she be the reason why,
    All the world for love may die.

          2. *How he saw her.*

    I beheld her, on a Day,
    When her looke out-flourisht May:
    And her dressing did out-brave°   *surpass in finery*
    All the Pride the fields than° have: *then*
5   Farre I was from being stupid,
    For I ran and call'd on *Cupid;*
    Love if thou wilt ever see
    Marke of glorie, come with me;
    Where's thy Quiver? bend thy Bow:
10 Here's a shaft, thou art to° slow!   *too*
    And (withall)° I did untie   *in addition*
    Every Cloud about his eye;
    But, he had not gain'd his sight
    Sooner, then° he lost his might,   *than*
15 Or his courage; for away
    Strait° hee ran, and durst not stay,   *straight: immediately*
    Letting Bow and Arrow fall,
    Nor for any threat, or Call,
    Could be brought once back to looke;
20 I foole-hardie, there up tooke
    Both the Arrow he had quit,°   *laid aside*
    And the Bow: with thought to hit
    This my object. But she threw
    Such a Lightning (as I drew)
25 At my face, that tooke my sight,
    And my motion from me quite;
    So that there, I stood a stone,
    Mock'd of all: and call'd of° one   *by*
    (Which with griefe and wrath I heard)
30 *Cupids* Statue with a Beard,
    Or else one that plaid his Ape,°   *imitated him (Cupid)*
    In a *Hercules*-his shape.

U-2.2.12 **Every ... eye**: in the Renaissance, Cupid is often represented as blindfolded
32 **Hercules-his**: archaic form of "Hercules's"; Hercules is traditionally represented as large and husky, as was Jonson at age fifty

3. *What hee suffered.*

After many scornes like these,
Which the prouder Beauties please,
She content was to restore
Eyes and limbes, to hurt me more;
5 And would on Conditions, be
Reconcil'd to Love,° and me: *Cupid*
First, that I must kneeling yeeld
Both the Bow, and shaft I held
Unto her; which Love might take
10 At her hand, with oath, to make
Mee, the scope of his next draught;° *drawing (of his bow)*
Aymed, with that selfe-same shaft
He no sooner heard the Law,° *decree (of Charis)*
But the Arrow home did draw
15 And (to gaine her by his Art)
Left it sticking in my heart:
Which when she beheld to bleed,
She repented of the deed,
And would faine° have chang'd the fate, *preferably, gladly*
20 But the Pittie comes too late.
Looser-like,° now, all my wreake° *like a loser/revenge*
Is, that I have leave to speake,
And in either Prose, or Song,
To revenge me with my Tongue,
25 Which how Dexterously I doe,
Heare and make Example too.

4. *Her Triumph.*

See the Chariot at hand here of Love
    Wherein my Lady rideth!
Each that drawes, is a Swan, or a Dove
    And well the Carre Love guideth;
5 As she goes, all hearts doe duty
    Unto her beauty,
And enamour'd, doe wish, so they might
    But enjoy such a sight,
That they still° were,° to run by her side, *always/were able*
10 Through Swords, through Seas, whether° she would ride. *wherever*

U-2.4.1–3 **Chariot . . . Dove**: Venus's chariot was traditionally drawn by swans or doves
10 **Through . . . through**: both pronounced as two syllables: "thorough"

> Doe but looke on her eyes, they doe light
> All that Loves world compriseth!
> Doe but looke on her Haire, it is bright
> As Loves starre° when it riseth!   *the planet Venus*
> 15 Doe but marke her forehead's smoother
> Then° words that sooth her!   *than*
> And from her arched browes, such a grace
> Sheds it selfe through the face,
> As alone there triumphs to the life
> 20 All the Gaine, all the Good, of the Elements strife.
>
> Have you seene but a bright Lillie grow,
> Before rude hands have touch'd it?
> Ha'you mark'd but the fall o'the Snow
> Before the soyle hath smutch'd° it?   *stained, blackened*
> 25 Ha'you felt the wooll of Bever?
> Or Swans Downe ever?
> Or have smelt o'the bud o'the Brier?
> Or the Nard° in the fire?   *spikenard: an aromatic root*
> Or have tasted the bag° of the Bee?   *where pollen is carried*
> 30 O so white! O so soft! O so sweet is she!

5. *His discourse with* Cupid.

> Noblest *Charis,* you that are
> Both my fortune, and my Starre!
> And doe governe more my blood,
> Then° the various° Moone the flood!°   *than/changeable/tides*
> 5 Heare, what late Discourse of you,
> Love, and I have had; and true.
> 'Mongst my Muses° finding me,   *inspirers and patronesses of his art*
> Where he chanc't your name to see
> Set, and to this softer straine;°   *tune, melody*
> 10 Sure, said he, if I have Braine,
> This here sung, can be no other
> By description, but my Mother!°   *Venus*
> So hath *Homer* prais'd her haire;
> So, *Anacreon* drawne the Ayre°   *expression*
> 15 Of her face, and made to rise
> Just about° her sparkling eyes,   *near*
> Both her Browes, bent like my Bow.
> By her lookes I doe her know,

---

20 **All ... strife**: the ancients believed that the divine harmony of the universe emerged from the warfare of the four elements: air, earth, fire, and water

U-2.5.13–14 ***Homer ... Anacreon***: two ancient Greek poets who extolled the beauty of Venus

	Which you call my Shafts. And see!	
20	Such my Mothers blushes be,	
	As the Bath° your verse discloses	*dye, color*
	In her cheekes, of Milke, and Roses;	
	Such as oft I wanton° in!	*play*
	And, above her even° chin,	*smooth*
25	Have you plac'd the banke of kisses,	
	Where you say, men gather blisses,	
	Rip'ned with a breath more sweet,	
	Then° when flowers, and West-winds meet.	*than*
	Nay, her white and polish'd neck,	
30	With the Lace that doth it deck,	
	Is my Mothers! Hearts of slaine	
	Lovers, made into a Chaine!	
	And betweene each rising breast,	
	Lyes the Valley, cal'd my nest,	
35	Where I sit and proyne° my wings	*prune: trim or dress feathers, preen*
	After flight; and put new stings°	*sharp points*
	To my shafts! Her very Name,	
	With my Mothers is the same.	
	I confesse all, I replide,	
40	And the Glasse° hangs by her side,	*mirror*
	And the Girdle 'bout her waste,°	*waist*
	All° is *Venus:* save° unchaste.	*all of Charis/except*
	But alas, thou seest the least	
	Of her good, who is the best	
45	Of her Sex; But could'st thou *Love,*	
	Call to mind the formes,° that strove	*ideal forms, goddesses*
	For the Apple, and those three	
	Make in one, the same were shee.	
	For this Beauty yet doth hide,	
50	Something more then° thou hast spi'd.	*than*
	Outward Grace° weake love beguiles:°	*physical beauty/deceives, deludes*
	Shee is *Venus,* when she smiles,	

37-38 Her ... same: in most of the ancient sources, including Homer's *Odyssey*, Vulcan's wife is named Venus; in the *Iliad*, however, she is named Charis; hence the two goddesses are sometimes conflated

40-41 Glasse ... Girdle: both are associated with Venus

42 All ... unchaste: Venus is the goddess of illicit love; Charis, as her name implies, is associated with divine, chaste love

46-47 formes ... Apple: alluding to the Judgment of Paris: Eris, the goddess of discord, angry at not being invited to an Olympian marriage feast, threw among the assembled goddesses a golden apple inscribed "For the fairest"; Juno (the stately queen of the gods), Minerva (the goddess of wisdom), and Venus all claimed the apple; the young Trojan prince Paris was made to judge among them; he awarded the apple to Venus, who had bribed him with the promise of the Greek queen Helen; his claiming of his payment brought about the Trojan War

52-54 Venus ... Minerva: see the note to lines 46-47

But shee's *Juno,* when she walkes,
And *Minerva,* when she talkes.

      6. *Clayming a second kisse by Desert.*

Charis guesse, and doe not misse,
Since I drew a Morning kisse
From your lips, and suck'd an ayre
Thence, as sweet, as you are faire,
5   What my Muse and I have done:
Whether we have lost, or wonne,
If by us, the oddes were laid,°   *a wager was placed*
That the Bride (allow'd° a Maid)°   *conceded to be/virgin*
Look'd not halfe so fresh, and faire,
10 With th'advantage of her haire,°   *down and bare, symbolizing virginity*
And her Jewels, to the view
Of th'Assembly, as did you!
    Or, that did you° sit, or walke,   *if you did*
You were more the eye,° and talke   *notice*
15 Of the Court, to day, then° all   *than*
Else that glister'd° in *White-hall;*°   *sparkled/the king's Westminster palace*
So, as those that had your sight,°   *had you in sight*
Wisht the Bride were chang'd to night,
And did thinke, such Rites were due
20 To no other Grace° but you!   *a goddess of beauty and charm*
    Or, if you did move to night
In the Daunces, with what spight°   *spite: envy*
Of your Peeres,° you were beheld,   *equals, here actually nobles*
That at every motion sweld
25 So to see a Lady tread,
As might all the Graces° lead,   *the three goddesses of beauty and charm*
And was worthy (being so seene)
To be envi'd of° the Queene.   *by*
    Or if you would yet have stay'd,°   *stopped (dancing)*
30 Whether any would up-braid
To himselfe his losse of Time;
Or have charg'd° his sight of Crime,   *accused*
To have left all sight° for you: *deserted all other sights*
    Guesse of these, which is the true;
35 And, if such a verse as this,
May not claime another kisse.

7. Begging another, on colour° of mending the former.   *pretense*

  For *Loves*-sake, kisse me once againe,
  I long,° and should not beg in vaine,   *long for: desire*
   Here's none to spie, or see;
    Why doe you doubt, or stay?°   *not act*
5   I'le taste° as lightly as the Bee,   *your lips*
  That doth but touch his flower, and flies away.
   Once more, and (faith)° I will be gone: *by my faith*
   Can he that loves, aske lesse then° one?   *than*
    Nay, you may erre in this,°   *the first kiss*
10   And all your bountie° wrong: *reputation for generosity*
  This could be call'd but halfe a kisse.
  What w'are but once to doe, we should doe long,°   *for a long time*
  I will but mend the last,° and tell   *kiss*
  Where, how it would have relish'd well;°   *have been well enjoyed (by me)*
15   Joyne lip to lip, and try:
    Each suck others breath.
  And whilst our tongues perplexed° lie,   *intertwined*
  Let who will thinke us dead, or wish our death.

8. Urging her of a promise.

 Charis one day in discourse
 Had of Love,° and of his force,   *on the subject of love*
 Lightly promis'd, she would tell
 What° a man she could love well: *what kind of*
5 And that promise set on fire
 All that heard her, with desire.
 With the rest, I long expected,°   *looked forward to*
 When the worke would be effected:
 But we find that cold delay,
10 And excuse spun every day,
 As, untill she tell her one,°   *describe her ideal man*
 We all feare, she loveth none.
 Therefore, *Charis,* you must do't,
 For I will so urge you to't
15 You shall neither eat, nor sleepe,
 No, nor forth your window peepe,
 With your emissarie° eye,   *messenger, agent*
 To fetch in the Formes° goe by: *shapes (of men) that*
 And pronounce, which band° or lace,°   *neckband, collar/at cuffs or collars*
20 Better fits him, then his face;
 Nay I will not let you sit

	'Fore your Idoll Glasse a whit,	
	To say over° every purle°	list/loop of lace
	There; or to reforme a curle;	
25	Or with Secretarie° *Sis*	confidential maid, lady's maid
	To consult, if *Fucus*° this	rouge, paint for the face
	Be as good, as was the last:	
	All your sweet of life° is past,	sweet time of life, idleness
	Make accompt° unlesse° you can,	an account, a list/if
30	(And that quickly) speake° your Man.°	describe/ideal man

    9. *Her man described by her owne Dictamen.°*   *dictate, pronouncement*

	Of your Trouble, *Ben,* to ease me,	
	I will tell what Man would please me.	
	I would have him if I could,	
	Noble; or of greater° Blood:	royal
5	Titles, I confesse, doe take° me;	captivate
	And a woman, God did make me.	
	French° to boote,° at least in fashion,	(he should be) French/as well
	And his Manners of that Nation.	
	Young I'ld have him to,° and faire,	too
10	Yet a man;° with crisped° haire	an adult, a masculine man/curled
	Cast in thousand snares, and rings	
	For *Loves* fingers, and his wings:	
	Chestnut colour, or more slack°	lighter, more varied
	Gold, upon a ground° of black.°	background/here, a darker color
15	*Venus,* and *Minerva's* eyes	
	For he must looke wanton-wise.	
	Eye-brows bent like *Cupids* bow,	
	Front,° an ample field of snow;	forehead
	Even° nose, and cheeke (withall)°	smooth, without blemish/in addition
20	Smooth as is the Billiard Ball:	
	Chin, as woolly as the Peach;	
	And his lip should kissing teach,	
	Till he cherish'd too much beard,	
	And make *Love* or me afeard.	
25	He would have a hand as soft	
	As the Downe, and shew it oft;	
	Skin as smooth as any rush,°	a marsh plant with smooth, pliant leaves
	And so thin to see a blush	
	Rising through it e're it came;°	before it arrived at the surface

---

U–2.8.22 **Idoll Glasse**: idolatrous mirror (worshiping your image)
U–2.9.15 ***Venus***: Venus's; she is the goddess of illicit, wanton love; ***Minerva's* eyes**: she is the goddess of wisdom; both had blue eyes
23 **Till . . . beard**: until he grew old enough to grow stiff whiskers

30	All his blood should be a flame	
	Quickly fir'd as in beginners	
	In loves schoole, and yet no sinners.°	*yet still virgins*
	'Twere to° long to speake of all,	*too*
	What we harmonie doe call	
35	In a body should be there.	
	Well he should his clothes to weare;	
	Yet no Taylor help° to make him	*tricks of a tailor, such as padding*
	Drest, you still° for man° should take° him;	*always/for a man/recognize*
	And not thinke h'had eat a stake,°	*hence be stiff in standing or moving*
40	Or were set up in a Brake.°	*be stiff in countenance, be expressionless*
	Valiant he should be as fire,	
	Shewing danger° more then° ire.°	*love of danger, bravery/than/anger*
	Bounteous as the clouds to earth;	
	And as honest as his Birth.	
45	All his actions to be such,	
	As to doe nothing too much.	
	Nor° o're-praise, nor yet condemne;	*neither*
	Nor° out-valew,° nor contemne;°	*neither/overvalue/despise, scorn*
	Nor° doe wrongs, nor wrongs receave;	*neither*
50	Nor° tie knots, nor knots unweave;	*neither*
	And from basenesse to be free,	
	As he durst° love Truth and me.	*dared*
	Such a man, with every part,	
	I could give my very heart;	
55	But of one,° if short he came,	*one part*
	I can rest me° where I am.	*cease, be at ease*

10. *Another Ladyes exception present at the hearing.*

	For his Mind, I doe not care,	
	That's a Toy, that I could spare:	
	Let his Title be but great,	
	His Clothes rich, and band° sit neat,	*neckband, collar*
5	Himselfe young, and face be good,	
	All I wish is understood:	
	What you please, you parts may call,	
	'Tis one good part I'ld lie withall.	

---

55 **if . . . came**: "if he lacked (one part)," with a bawdy play—by the poet if not by Charis—on "if his one part came up short"
U-2.10.8 **I'ld . . . withall**: bawdy pun on "I would rest (cease) despite (all your other requirements)" and "I would lie with"

[U-4]   A SONG.

    Oh doe not wanton° with those eyes,   *play lasciviously*
        Lest I be sick with seeing;
    Nor cast them downe, but let them rise,
        Lest shame destroy their being:
5   O, be not angry with those fires,
        For then their threats will kill me;
    Nor looke too kind on my desires,
        For then my hopes will spill° me;   *destroy, with a pun on ejaculate*
    O, doe not steepe them in thy Teares,
10   For so will sorrow slay me;
    Nor spread° them as distract with feares,   *open widely*
        Mine owne° enough betray me.   *fears*

[U-9]   *My Picture left in* Scotland.

    I now thinke, Love is rather deafe, then° blind,   *than*
        For else it could not be,
                That she,
    Whom I adore so much, should so slight me,
5   And cast my love behind:
    I'm sure my language to her, was as sweet,
               And every close° did meet   *concluding (musical) phrase*
            In sentence,° of as subtile feet,°   *substance, meaning/measure*
            As hath° the youngest Hee,   *has (that poetry by)*
10   That sits in shadow of *Apollo's* tree.
    Oh, but my conscious feares,
        That flie my thoughts betweene,
        Tell me that she hath seene
        My hundreds of gray haires,
15   Told° seven and fortie yeares,   *counted (my)*
    Read so much wast,° as she cannot imbrace   *waist, waste*
    My mountaine belly, and my rockie° face,   *pitted, unsmooth*
    And all these through her eyes, have stopt° her eares.   *stopped up*

U-9.title **Scotland**: Jonson made a walking trip to Scotland in 1618–19, when he was in his mid-forties; he sent a copy of this poem to one of his Scottish hosts, William Drummond of Hawthornden, on 19 January 1619 (*Conversations* 660–78)
1 **blind**: Cupid is often presented as blindfolded
10 *Apollo's* **tree**: the laurel, symbol of poetic achievement

[U-14] TO HIS HONORD FRIEND Mʳ JOHN SELDEN.

    I know to whome I write: Here, I am sure,
    Though I be short,° I cannot be obscure.°   *brief/open to misunderstanding*
    Lesse shall I for the art,° or dressing° care;   *artifice/poetic flourishes*
    Since, naked, best *Truth*, and the *Graces* are.
5 Your Booke, my *Selden*, I have read; and much
    Was trusted, that you thought my judgment such
    To aske it: though, in most of Workes,° it be   *in (reading) most works*
    A penance,° where a man may not be free,   *punishment*
    Rather then° office.° When it doth, or may   *than/pleasant obligation*
10 Chance, that the Friends affection proves allay
    Unto the censure. Yours° all need doth flye   *your work*
    Of this so vitious humanitie:°   *characteristic of human behavior*
    Then° which, there is not unto *Studie*'a° more   *than/scholarship a*
    Pernicious enemie. Wee see, before
15 A many' of Bookes, even good judgments wound
    Themselves, through favoring° that,° is there not found: *praising/what*
    But I to yours, farre from this fault, shall doo;
    Not flye° the crime, but the suspicion too.   *not only flee from*
    Though I confesse (as every Muse hath err'd,
20 And mine not least) I have too oft preferr'd°   *raised*
    Men past their termes; and prais'd some names too much:
    But 'twas, with purpose, to have made them such.°   *as I described them*
    Since,° being deceiv'd, I turne a sharper eye   *since then*
    Upon my selfe; and aske, to whome, and why,
25 And what I write: and vexe° it manie dayes,   *debate, worry over*
    Before men get a verse,° much lesse a prayse.   *poem (from me)*
    So, that my Reader is assur'd, I now
    Meane what I speake; and, still,° will keepe that vow.   *always*
        Stand forth my object, then. You, that have been
30 Ever° at home, yet have all Countries seene;°   *always/through study*
    And, like a Compasse, keeping one foot still
    Upon your center, do your circle fill
    Of generall knowledge; watch'd men; manners too;
    Heard, what past times have said; seen, what ours do;

U-14.title **JOHN SELDEN**: noted jurist and antiquarian (1584–1654), author of many books, including *Titles of Honor* (1614), to which this poem was prefaced
4 **naked ... are**: both *Truth* and the three *Graces*, goddesses of beauty and charm, are traditionally pictured naked
5 **Your Booke**: *Titles of Honor*, a historical study of royal and honorific titles
8 **be free**: to speak truthfully
10–11 **allay ... censure**: alloy to the criticism; that is, keeps the critic from speaking freely of his friend's work
14–15 **before ... Bookes**: in commendatory poems prefacing a great number of books
21 **termes**: limitations

35 Which *Grace* shall I make love to first? your skill?
    Or faith in things?° Or, is't your wealth,° and will   *facts/of knowledge*
    To informe, and teach? Or, your unwearied paine
    Of gath'ring?° Bountie'in pouring out againe?   *gathering information*
    What *Fables* have you vex'd!° What Truth redeemd!   *puzzled over*
40 Antiq'uities search'd! Opinions disesteem'd!
    Impostures branded, and Authorities urg'd!
    What Blots and Errors have you watch'd,° and purg'd   *perceived*
    Records and *Authors* of! How rectified°   *reformed*
    Times, Manners, Customes! Innovations spied!
45 Sought out the Fountaines, Sources, Creekes, Paths, Wayes!
    And noted the Beginnings, and Decayes!
    Where is that nominall Marke, or reall Rite,
    Forme, Art, or Ensigne,° that hath scap'd your sight?   *banner, flag*
    How are Traditions there examin'd! How
50 Conjectures retriv'd!° And a Storie, now   *from their former obscurity*
    And then, of times (beside the bare conduct
    Of what it tells us) weav'd in, to instruct!
    I wonder'd at the richnesse: but, am lost,
    To see the workmanship so exceed the cost.
55 To marke the excellent seas'nings of your stile,
    And masculine elocution; not one while°   *at one point*
    With horror rough, then° rioting with wit;   *at another point*
    But, to the subject, still° the colours fit: *always*
    In sharpnesse of all search, wisdome of choice,
60 Newnesse of sense, antiquitie of voice.
    I yeeld, I yeeld. The Matter of your prayse
    Flowes in upon me; and I cannot rayse
    A banke against it: Nothing, but the round
    Large claspe of *Nature*, such a wit° can bound.°   *cleverness/encompass*
65 *Monarch* in *Letters!* 'Mongst thy *Titles* showne,
    Of others *Honors;* thus, enjoy thine owne.
    I, first, salute thee so: and gratulate,°   *hail, salute*
    With that thy Style, thy keeping of thy State,°   *manner of living*
    In offring this thy Worke to no *Great Name;*
70 That would perhaps have prais'd, and thank'd the same,
    But nought beyond. He, thou hast giv'n it to,

---

47 **nominall Mark**: naming feature, token sign; here contrasted with a **reall Rite** (an actually existing ceremony)

58 **to ... fit**: the rhetorical figures of speech (**colours**) are always appropriate to the subject matter

61 **Matter ... prayse**: the (copious) reasons for praising you

64 **Large ... Nature**: the whole of creation

69 **offring ... Name**: *Titles of Honor* was not dedicated to a nobleman, in hopes of patronage, but to Selden's **learned Chamber-fellow (72)** at the Inner Temple, Edward **Heyward (81)** or Hayward (died 1658), a fellow lawyer and a minor poet

Thy learned Chamber-fellow, knowes to do
It true respects. He will, not only, love,
Embrace, and cherish; but, he can approve° *confirm*
75 And estimate thy paines: as having wrought° *worked*
In the rich mines of knowledge, and thence brought
Humanitie inough, to be a Friend,
And strength, to be a Champion, and defend
Thy gift'gainst Envie. O, how I doe count
80 Amongst my commings in (and see it mount)
The gaine of two such Friendships; *Heyward,* and
Selden, two *Names,* that so much understand:
On whome, I could take up° (and nere° abuse° *get/ ne'er: never/wrong*
The credit)° what° would furnish a tenth *Muse.* *believability/that which*
85 But here's nor° time, nor place, my wealth to tell; *neither*
You both are modest: so am I. Farewell.

[U-22]   *An Elegie.*

Though Beautie be the Marke° of praise, *target*
   And yours of whom I sing be such
   As not the World can praise too much,
Yet is't your vertue now I raise.

5 A vertue, like Allay,° so gone *alloy*
   Throughout your forme; as° though that° move, *that/your beauty*
   And draw, and conquer all mens love,
This° subjects you to love of one. *your vertue*

Wherein you triumph yet: because
10   'Tis of your selfe, and that you use
   The noblest freedome, not to chuse
Against or° Faith, or honours lawes. *either*

But who should lesse expect from you,
   In whom alone love° lives agen? *Love: Cupid*
15   By whom he is restor'd to men:
And kept, and bred,° and brought up true?° *trained/to ideals*

---

80 my commings in: income, the rewards of my life
84 tenth *Muse*: the nine classical Muses were patrons and inspirers of the arts
85 my . . . tell: my wealth (in having two such friends) to relate (and to count)

His falling Temples you have rear'd,
    The withered Garlands tane° away;   *taken*
    His Altars kept from the Decay,
20 That envie wish'd, and Nature fear'd.

And on them burne so chaste a flame,
    With so much Loyalties° expence   *faithfulness's*
    As Love t'aquit° such excellence,   *to reward*
Is gone himselfe into your Name.

25 And you are he: the Dietie
    To whom all Lovers are design'd;°   *appointed*
    That would their better objects° find: *ideals, patterns*
Among which faithfull troope am I.

Who as an off-spring at your shrine,
30   Have sung this Hymne, and here intreat
    One sparke of your Diviner heat
To light upon a Love of mine.

Which if it kindle not, but scant°   *sparingly*
    Appeare, and that to shortest view,°   *for a short time*
35   Yet give me leave t'adore in you
What I, in her, am griev'd to want.°   *lack*

[U-38]   *An Elegie.*

'Tis true, I'm broke! Vowes, Oathes, and all I had
    Of Credit lost. And I am now run madde:
Or doe upon my selfe some desperate ill;
    This sadnesse makes no approaches, but to kill.
5 It is a Darknesse hath blockt up my sense,
    And drives it in to eat on my offence,
Or there to sterve° it; helpe O you that may   *starve, destroy*
    Alone lend succours,° and this furie stay,°   *succor: assistance/stop*
Offended Mistris, you are yet so faire,
10   As light breakes from you, that affrights despaire,
And fills my powers with perswading joy,
    That you should be too noble to destroy.
There may some face or menace of a storme
    Looke forth, but cannot last in such forme.

U-22.24 Is ... name: the four letters making up "love" are in your name; Lady Covell, to whom Jonson wrote a verse epistle (U-56, not in this collection), has been suggested as the person addressed in this elegy; nothing is known of her beyond her name
U-38: it is likely that U-38, U-40, and U-41 form a sequence

15 If there be nothing worthy you can see
         Of Graces,° or your mercie here in me,   *favors (from you)*
     Spare your owne goodnesse yet; and be not great
         In will and power, only to defeat.
     God, and the good, know to forgive, and save.
20   The ignorant, and fooles, no pittie have.
     I will not stand to justifie my fault,
         Or lay the excuse upon the Vintners vault;°   *that is, on being drunk*
     Or in confessing of the Crime be nice,°   *reluctant, unwilling*
         Or goe about to countenance the vice,
25   By naming in what companie 'twas in,
         As° I would urge Authoritie for sinne.   *as if*
     No, I will stand arraign'd, and cast,° to be   *found guilty*
         The Subject of your Grace° in pardoning me,   *favor*
     And (Stil'd° your mercies Creature)° will live more   *called/product*
30   Your honour now, then° your disgrace before;   *than*
     Thinke it was frailtie, Mistris, thinke me man,
         Thinke that your selfe like heaven forgive me can,
     Where weaknesse doth offend, and vertue grieve,
         There greatnesse takes a glorie to relieve.
35   Thinke that I once was yours, or may be now,
         Nothing is vile, that is a part of you:
     Errour and folly in me may have crost
         Your just commands; yet those, not I be lost.
     I am regenerate now, become the child
40   Of your compassion; Parents should be mild:
     There is no Father that for one demerit,
         Or two, or three, a Sonne will dis-inherit,
     That° as the last of punishments is meant;   *disinheritance*
         No man inflicts that paine, till hope be spent:
45   An ill-affected limbe (what e're° it aile)   *e'er: ever*
         We cut not off, till all Cures else doe faile:
     And then with pause; for sever'd once, that's gone,
         Would live his glory that could keepe it on:
     Doe not despaire° my mending; to distrust   *despair of*
50   Before you prove° a medicine, is unjust;   *try, test*
     You may so place me, and in such an ayre
         As° not alone the Cure, but scarre be faire.° *that/the scar looks good*
     That is, if still° your Favours you apply,   *as yet, always*
         And not the bounties you ha' done, deny.
55   Could you demand° the gifts you gave, againe!   *order the return of*
         Why was't? did e're° the Cloudes aske back their raine?   *ever (before)*
     The Sunne his heat, and light, the ayre his dew?
         Or winds the Spirit, by which the flower so grew?

---

21 **my fault**: the speaker has betrayed the lady's confidence

That were to wither all, and make a Grave
60   Of that° wise Nature would a Cradle have!   *that which*
Her order is to cherish, and preserve,
    Consumptions nature to° destroy, and sterve.°   *(is) to/starve, kill*
But to exact againe what once is given,
    Is natures meere° obliquitie!° as° Heaven   *absolute/aberration/as if*
65   Should aske° the blood, and spirits he° hath infus'd   *call back/God*
In man, because man hath the flesh abus'd.
O may your wisdome take example hence,
    God lightens° not at mans each fraile offence,   *emits lightning flashes*
He pardons slips, goes by° a world of ills,   *passes over*
70   And then his thunder frights more, then° it kills.   *than*
He cannot angrie be, but° all must quake,   *unless*
    It shakes even him, that all things else doth shake.
And how more faire, and lovely lookes the world
    In a calme skie, then° when the heaven is horl'd°   *than/hurled*
75 About in Cloudes, and wrapt in raging weather,
    As° all with storme and tempest ran together.   *as though*
O imitate that sweet Serenitie
    That makes us live, not that which calls to die;
In darke, and sullen mornes, doe we not say
80   This looketh like an Execution day?
And with the vulgar° doth it not obtaine   *uneducated people*
    The name of Cruell weather, storme, and raine?
Be not affected with these markes° too much   *signs*
    Of crueltie, lest they doe make you such.
85 But view the mildnesse of your Makers state,
    As I the penitents here emulate:
He° when he sees a sorrow such as this,   *God*
    Streight° puts off all his Anger, and doth kisse   *without delay*
The contrite Soule, who hath no thought to win
90   Upon the hope to have another sin
Forgiven him; And in that lyne stand I
    Rather then° once displease you more, to die,   *than*
To suffer tortures, scorne, and Infamie,
    What° Fooles, and all their Parasites can apply;   *whatever*
95 The wit of Ale, and *Genius* of the Malt
    Can pumpe° for; or a Libell without salt°   *work/wit, sting*
Produce; though threatning with a coale, or chalke
    On every wall, and sung where e're I walke.
I number these as being of the Chore°   *chorus*
100   Of Contumelie,° and urge a good man more   *contemptuous insult*
Then° sword, or fire, or what is of the race°   *than/similar kind*
    To carry° noble danger° in the face: *bear, express/bravery*

---

97 with . . . chalke: by being written in charcoal or chalk

There is not any punishment, or paine,
    A man should flie from, as he would disdaine.°   *(from) disdain*
105 Then Mistris here, here let your rigour° end,   *severe strictness*
    And let your mercie make me asham'd t'offend.
I will no more abuse my vowes to you,
    Then° I will studie falshood, to° be true.   *than/in order to*
O, that you could but by dissection see
110   How much you are the better part of me;
How all my Fibres by your Spirit doe move,
    And that there is no life in me, but love.
You would be then most confident, that tho
    Publike affaires command me now to goe
115 Out of your eyes, and be awhile away;
    Absence, or Distance, shall not breed decay.
Your forme shines here, here fixed in my heart;
    I may dilate° my selfe, but not depart.   *expand, extend*
Others by common Stars their courses run,
120   When I see you, then I doe see my Sun,
Till then 'tis all but darknesse, that I have;
    Rather then° want° your light, I wish a grave.   *than/lack, do without*

[U-40]   *An Elegie.*

That Love's a bitter sweet, I ne're conceive
    Till the sower° Minute comes of taking leave,   *sour*
And then I taste it. But as men drinke up
    In hast° the bottome of a med'cin'd Cup,   *haste*
5 And take some sirrup° after; so doe I   *sweet drink*
    To put all relish° from my memorie   *distinctive flavor*
Of parting, drowne it in the hope to meet
    Shortly againe: and make our absence sweet.
This makes me, Mistris, that sometime by stealth,
10   Under another Name, I take° your health;   *drink to*
And turne the Ceremonies of those Nights
    I give, or owe my friends, into your Rites,
But ever without blazon,° or least shade°   *description, show/shadow, hint*
    Of vowes so sacred, and in silence made;
15 For though Love thrive, and may grow up with cheare,
    And free societie, hee's borne else-where,
And must be bred,° so to conceale his birth,   *educated, trained*
    As neither wine doe rack° it out, or mirth.   *draw (by torture)*
Yet should the Lover still° be ayrie and light   *always*
20   In all his Actions rarified to spright;°   *spirit*

U-40: see the note to U-38

  Not like a *Midas* shut up in himselfe,
    And turning all he toucheth into pelfe,°   *riches*
  Keepe in reserv'd in his Dark-lanterne face,
    As if that ex'lent° Dulnesse were Loves grace;   *excellent*
25 No Mistris no, the open merrie Man
    Moves like a sprightly River, and yet can
  Keepe secret in his Channels what he breedes°   *accomplishes*
    'Bove° all your standing waters, choak'd with weedes.   *more than*
  They looke at best like Creame-bowles, and you soone
30   Shall find their depth: they're sounded° with a spoone.   *measured*
  They may say Grace, and for Loves Chaplaines passe;
    But the grave° Lover ever was an Asse;   *morose, sad faced*
  Is fix'd upon one leg, and dares not come°   *step*
    Out° with the other, for hee's still° at home;   *ahead/always*
35 Like the dull wearied Crane that (come on land)
    Doth while he keepes his watch, betray his stand.
  Where° he that knowes will like a Lapwing flie   *whereas*
    Farre from the Nest, and so himselfe belie°   *tell lies*
  To others as he will deserve the Trust
40   Due to that one, that doth believe him just.
  And such your Servant is, who vowes to keepe
    The Jewell of your name, as close° as sleepe   *secret*
  Can lock the Sense up, or the heart a thought,
    And never be by time, or folly brought,
45 Weaknesse of braine, yet no sinners.°   *yet still virgins*
    The sinne of Boast, or other countermine
  (Made to blow up loves secrets) to discover
    That Article, may° not become° our lover: *which may/be appropriate to*
  Which in assurance to your brest I tell,
50   If° I had writ no word, but Deare, farewell.   *as if*

[U-41]   *An Elegie.*

  Since you must goe, and I must bid farewell,
    Heare Mistris, your departing servant tell
  What it is like: And doe not thinke they can
    Be idle words, though of a parting Man;°   *man parting (from you)*

---

21 **Midas**: mythical king who was given the power to turn everything he touched into gold
23 **Dark-lanterne**: a lantern with a flap or slide that can be closed to conceal its light
36 **betray . . . stand**: betray where he is nesting; cranes are notoriously noisy
37 **knowes**: how to love properly, appropriately
37–38 **Lapwing . . . Nest**: faced with a predator, the lapwing flies away from her nest to protect her brood
40 **one . . . just**: that is, his mistress
U-41: see the note to U-38

68

  5   It is as if a night should shade noone-day,
         Or that the Sun was here, but forc't away;
     And we were left under that Hemisphere
         Where we must feele it Darke for halfe a yeere.
     What fate is this to change mens dayes and houres,
10   To shift their seasons, and destroy their powers!
     Alas I ha' lost my heat, my blood, my prime,
         Winter is come a Quarter e're° his Time,   *three months before*
     My health will leave me; and when you depart,
         How shall I doe sweet Mistris for my heart?,
15   You would restore it? No, that's worth a feare,
         As if it were not worthy to be there:
     O, keepe it still;° for it had rather be   *as yet, always*
         Your sacrifice,° then° here remaine with me.   *my sacrifice to you/than*
     And so I spare it: Come what can become
20   Of me, I'le softly tread unto my Tombe;
     Or like a Ghost walke silent amongst men,
         Till I may see both it and you agen.

[U-42]   *An Elegie.*

     Let me be what I am, as *Virgil* cold
         As *Horace* fat; or as *Anacreon* old;
     No Poets verses yet did ever move,
         Whose Readers did not thinke he° was in love.   *the poet*
  5   Who shall forbid me then in Rithme° to bee   *rhythm: poetry*
         As light, and Active as the youngest hee°   *man*
     That from the Muses fountaines doth indorse°   *confirm, certify*
         His lynes, and hourely sits° the Poets horse?°   *sits on/winged Pegasus*
     Put on my Ivy Garland,° let me see   *poet's crown*
10   Who frownes, who jealous is, who taxeth me.
     Fathers, and Husbands, I doe claime a right
         In all that is call'd lovely: take my sight
     Sooner then° my affection from the faire.   *than*
         No face, no hand, proportion, line, or Ayre
15   Of beautie; but the Muse hath interest in:
         There is not worne that lace, purle,° knot or pin,   *loop of fabric*
     But is° the Poëts matter:° And he must   *that escapes being/subject*
         When he is furious° love, although not lust.   *in a poetic frenzy*

---

14 **for ... heart**: that is, without a heart (since my heart goes along with you)
U-42.1–2 **Virgil ... old**: the Roman historian Suetonius so describes the poets Virgil and Horace; the Greek historian Lucian so describes the poet Anacreon
7 **Muses fountaines**: sources of inspiration
15 **but ... in**: that is, escapes the interest of the Muse

69

	But then content,° your Daughters and your Wives,	*be contented*
20	(If they be faire and worth it) have their lives	
	Made longer by our praises. Or, if not,	
	Wish you had fowle ones, and deformed got;	
	Curst in their Cradles, or there chang'd° by Elves,	*exchanged, altered*
	So to be sure you doe injoy your selves.	
25	Yet keepe° those up in sackcloth° too, or lether,	*dress/coarse fabric*
	For Silke will draw some sneaking Songster thither.	
	It is a ryming Age, and Verses swarme	
	At every stall;° The Cittie Cap's a charme.	*peddlar's stall*
	But I who live, and have liv'd twentie yeare	
30	Where I may handle Silke,° as free, and neere,	*that is, at court*
	As any Mercer;° or the whale-bone man	*cloth merchant*
	That quilts those bodies, I have leave to span:	
	Have eaten with the Beauties, and the wits,	
	And braveries° of Court, and felt their fits	*finely dressed persons*
35	Of love, and hate: and came so nigh° to know°	*near/as to discover*
	Whether their faces were their owne, or no.	
	It is not likely I should now looke downe	
	Upon a Velvet Petticote,° or a Gowne,	*skirt*
	Whose like I have knowne the Taylors Wife put on	
40	To doe her Husbands rites in, e're 'twere gone	
	Home to the Customer: his Letcherie°	*lustful fantasy*
	Being, the best clothes still° to præoccupie.	*always*
	Put a Coach-mare° in Tissue,° must I horse°	*work horse/fine cloth/mount*
	Her presently?° Or leape° thy Wife of force,	*immediately/mount*
45	When by thy sordid bountie she hath on,	
	A Gowne of that, was the Caparison?	
	So° I might dote upon thy Chaires and Stooles	*just as*
	That are like° cloath'd, must I be of those fooles	*similarly*
	Of race° accompted,° that no passion have	*that kind/accounted*
50	But when thy Wife (as thou conceiv'st) is brave?	

---

24 **you . . . selves**: only you could enjoy them (because they appear ugly to others)
28 **The . . . charme**: the badge of being a city dweller is an amulet (that causes all who have one to write verses)
31–32 **whale-bone . . . bodies**: whale bones were used to make the hoops for skirts that "quilted" (padded out) the natural shape of the body
32 **leave . . . span**: permission to encircle with my hands (the cloth, and perhaps the bodies under it)
36 **Whether . . . owne**: whether they were what they appeared to be; glancing at the duplicity of courtiers
37–38 **looke . . . Upon**: take notice of
40 **doe . . . rites**: have sexual intercourse with her husband
42 **præoccupie**: use in advance of delivery to the buyer; "occupy" also means to use sexually
44 **of force**: perforce, necessarily
46 **was . . . Caparison**: which was actually an ornamental cloth draped over a horse
50 **brave**: finely dressed, proud, vain

Then ope thy wardrobe, thinke me that poore Groome
   That from the Foot-man, when he was become
An Officer there, did make most solemne love,
   To ev'ry Petticote he brush'd, and Glove
55 He did lay up,° and would adore the shooe,   *put into storage*
   Or slipper was° left off, and kisse it too,   *that was*
Court every hanging Gowne, and after that,
   Lift up some one, and doe, I tell not what.
Thou didst tell me; and wert o're-joy'd to peepe
60   In at a hole, and see these Actions creepe
From the poore wretch, which though he play'd in prose,
   He would have done in verse, with° any of those   *along with*
Wrung on the Withers, by Lord Loves despight,°   *contempt*
   Had he had the facultie to reade, and write!
65 Such Songsters there are store° of; witnesse he   *a large number*
   That chanc'd the lace, laid on a Smock, to see
And straight-way spent° a Sonnet; with that other   *uttered, ejaculated*
   That (in pure Madrigall) unto his Mother
Commended the French-hood, and Scarlet gowne
70   The Lady Mayresse° pass'd in through the Towne,   *mayor's wife*
Unto the Spittle Sermon. O, what strange
   Varietie of Silkes were on th'Exchange!
Or in Moore-fields! this other night, sings one,
   Another answers, 'Lasse° those Silkes are none°   *Alas/nothing*
75 In smiling *L'envoye,*° as° he would deride   *a concluding stanza/as if*
   Any Comparison had with his Cheap-side.
And vouches° both the Pageant, and the Day,   *attests to*
   When not the Shops, but windowes doe display
The Stuffes,° the Velvets, Plushes, Fringes, Lace,   *materials*
80   And all the originall riots of the place:
Let the poore fooles enjoy their follies, love
   A Goat in Velvet; or some block could move
Under that cover; an old Mid-wives hat!

52–53 become ... there: when he was put in charge of his mistress's wardrobe
63 Wrung Withers: distressed, pained, literally pinched between the shoulders (as a horse is by a tight saddle)
68 Madrigall: song for two or more voices
71 Spittle Sermon: preached during Easter Week near the Hospital of St. Mary, Bishopsgate Without, attended by City of London dignitaries
72 th'Exchange: the new Exchange on the Strand, a building filled with fashionable shops
73 Moore-fields: Moorfields, a marshy area north of London where the city's laundresses dried clothing
76 Cheap-side: an area where cloth (particularly silk) merchants had their shops
77–80 both ... place: for pageants and other special occasions, the citizens hung cloth banners, in a riot of colors, from their windows
82–83 Goat: a lecherous person; **block:** blockhead, a continent person; **Under that cover:** wearing that hat, in that disguise (blockheads are literally wooden heads used for shaping or storing hats)

chamber pot/dressed up

Or a Close-stoole° so cas'd;° or any fat
85 Bawd,° in a Velvet scabberd!° I envy loose woman/covering
   None of their pleasures! nor will aske thee, why
  Thou art jealous of thy Wifes, or Daughters Case:° clothing
   More then° of eithers manners, wit, or face! than

[U-47]   *An Epistle answering to one that asked to be*
          Sealed of the Tribe of BEN.

Men that are safe, and sure, in all they doe,
  Care not what trials they are put unto;
They meet the fire, the Test, as Martyrs would;
  And though Opinion stampe them not, are gold.
5 I could say more of such, but that I flie° avoid (by flying away)
  To speake my selfe out too ambitiously,
And shewing so weake an Act to vulgar° eyes, common, uninitiated
  Put conscience and my right to comprimise.
Let those that meerely talke, and never thinke,
10   That live in the wild Anarchie of Drinke
Subject to quarrell only; or else such
  As make it their proficiencie, how much
They'ave glutted in, and letcher'd out that weeke,
  That never yet did friend, or friendship seeke
15 But° for a Sealing: let these men protest. except
  Or th'other on their borders,° that will jeast near them (in conduct)
On° all Soules that are absent; even the dead about
  Like flies, or wormes, which mans corrupt parts fed:
That to speake well, thinke it above all sinne,° the highest sin
20   Of any Companie but° that° they are in, except/that which
Call every night to Supper in these fitts,° of malicious criticism
  And are receiv'd for° the Covey° of Witts; accepted as/small group
That censure all the Towne, and all th'affaires,
  And know whose ignorance is more then° theirs; than
25 Let these men have their wayes, and take their times
  To vent their Libels, and to issue rimes,
I have no portion in them, nor their deale
  Of newes they get, to strew out° the long meale, scatter throughout
I studie other friendships, and more one,° truer
30   Then° these can ever be; or else wish none. than

U-47.title: Jonson's followers in poetry were referred to as the **Tribe** or the Sons of Ben, the former alluding to Revelation 7, where four angels "seal," with marks on their foreheads, those to be saved from the twelve tribes of Israel: "Of the tribe of Benjamin were sealed twelve thousand" (v. 8); here, to seal is to initiate, as into an exclusive fraternity; the poem was written in 1623

8 comprimise: into a compromised position

>
> What is't to me whether the French Designe°   *plan, policy*
>   Be, or be not, to get the *Val-telline?*
> Or the States° Ships sent forth belike° to meet   *Dutch/perhaps*
>   Some hopes of *Spaine* in their West-Indian Fleet?
> 35 Whether the Dispensation yet be sent,
>   Or that the Match from *Spaine* was ever meant?
> I wish all well, and pray high heaven conspire
>   My Princes safetie, and my Kings desire,
> But if for honour, we must draw the Sword,
> 40   And force back that, which will not be restor'd,
> I have a body, yet, that spirit drawes
>   To live, or fall, a Carkasse in the cause.
> So farre without inquirie what the States,
>   *Brunsfield,* and *Mansfield* doe this yeare, my fates
> 45 Shall carry me at Call; and I'le be well,
>   Though I doe neither heare these newes, nor tell
> Of *Spaine* or *France;* or were not prick'd downe° one   *checked off as*
>   Of the late Mysterie of reception,
> Although my Fame, to his,° not under-heares,°   *Jones's/is not inferior*
> 50   That° guides the Motions, and directs the beares.   *who*
> But that's a blow, by which in time I may
>   Lose all my credit with my Christmas Clay,
> And animated *Porc'lane* of the Court,
>   I,° and for this neglect, the courser° sort   *aye: yes/coarser*

---

32 Val-telline: a strategic valley in Lombardy, held by the Spanish from 1621 to 1623, then the French from 1624 to 1627

34 hopes . . . Fleet: the Spanish fleet bringing back treasure from the West Indies

35-36 Dispensation . . . Spaine: a dispensation from the Pope was needed for the projected marriage of England's Protestant Prince Charles to the Roman Catholic Spanish Infanta; in England, the negotiations were popularly called the Spanish Match; they were broken off without success in 1623

38 Princes safetie: at the time this poem was written, Prince Charles was in Spain, wooing the princess

40 force . . . restor'd: take back by force that which will not otherwise be restored, a reference to the conquest of the Protestant German Palatinate in the early 1620s by the forces of the Roman Catholic Emperor and the Spanish crown; Frederick, the Prince Palatine, was married to the English princess Elizabeth, and many Englishmen, Jonson obviously among them (see lines 41-42), thought that King James should send troops to restore his son in law's dominion

43-44 States: the Low Countries, sympathetic to Frederick; **Brunsfield**: probably Christian of Brunswick, who fought on Frederick's side; **Mansfield**: the commander of Frederick's forces

48 late . . . reception: recent committee formed to arrange a reception for the Spanish Infanta at Southampton; Jonson's former collaborator in producing court masques but now rival and enemy, the set designer and architect Inigo Jones (1573-1652), was a member of that committee, probably accounting for Jonson's exclusion from it

50 guides . . . beares: a contemptuous reference to Jones as one who merely **guides the Motions** of puppets and directs bear baitings

52-53 Lose . . . Court: because of Jones's influence at court, Jonson fears losing his own position there as writer of entertainments and masques for the Christmas revels, his **Christmas Clay** (52)

54-55 courser . . . Jarres: another contemptuous reference to Jones, whose work Jonson deems earthenware when compared to his own *Porc'lane* (53)

<pre>
55   Of earthen Jarres, there may molest me too:
        Well, with mine owne fraile Pitcher, what to doe
     I have decreed; keepe it from waves, and presse;°   crowds
        Lest it be justled, crack'd, made nought, or lesse:
     Live to that point° I will; for which I am man,   purpose
60   And dwell as° in my Center, as I can   as much
     Still° looking too,° and ever loving heaven;   always/to
        With reverence using all the gifts then given.
     'Mongst which, if I have any friendships sent
        Such as are square, wel-tagde, and permanent,
65   Not built with Canvasse, paper, and false° lights   painted, not real
        As are the Glorious Scenes, at the great sights;
     And that there be no fev'ry heats, nor colds,
        Oylie Expansions, or shrunke durtie folds,
     But all so cleare, and led by reasons flame,
70   As but to stumble in her sight were shame.
     These I will honour, love, embrace, and serve:
        And free it° from all question to preserve.°   friendship/endure
     So short° you read my Character, and theirs°   in brief/theirs whom
        I would call mine, to which not many Staires
75   Are asked to climbe. First give me faith, who know
        My selfe a little. I will take° you so,°   accept/in the same manner
     As you have writ your selfe. Now stand, and then
        Sir, you are Sealed of the Tribe of Ben.
</pre>

[U-49]   *An Epigram on The Court Pucell.*

<pre>
     Do's the Court-Pucell then so censure me,
        And thinkes I dare not her? let the world see.
     What though her Chamber be the very pit
        Where fight the prime Cocks of the Game, for wit?
5   And that as any are strooke,° her breath creates   struck out, excluded
        New in their stead, out of the Candidates?
     What though with Tribade° lust she force a Muse,   lesbian
</pre>

56–58 Pitcher . . . crack'd: alluding to "the pitcher be broken at the fountain" (Ecclesiastes 12:6), a metaphor for dying
60 dwell . . . Center: Jonson's impressa (seal) was a broken compass with the circle left incomplete
62 With . . . given: a reference to the parable of the talents, Matthew 25:14–30
64 wel-tagde: well-tagged: well knit
65–66 Not . . . sights: a reference to the elaborate but impermanent scenery of the court masques; another jibe at Jones
68 Oylie . . . folds: as found on canvas scenery
U-49.title Pucell: Jonson plays here on contradictory meanings of the word, maid (virgin) and slut; *Conversations* 103–104 and 646–48 identify her as Cecilia Bulstrode (1584–1609), a friend of Lucy Countess of Bedford, who nursed her through her painful last illness; John Donne and Lucy exchanged elegies on her death; and Jonson, perhaps in amends for this epigram, wrote an admiring elegy praising her and her virginity (not in this collection)

       And in an Epicæne fury can write newes
       Equall with that, which for the best newes goes
10   As aërie light, and as like wit as those?°   *of the male wits*
       What though she talke, and cannot° once with them,   *cannot but at*
          Make State, Religion, Bawdrie, all a theame?
       And as lip-thirstie, in each words expence,
          Doth labour with the Phrase more then the sense?
15   What though she ride two mile on Holy-dayes
          To Church, as others doe to Feasts and Playes,
       To shew their Tires?° to view, and to be view'd?   *attires: clothes*
       What though she be with Velvet gownes indu'd,°   *clothed*
       And spangled Petticotes° brought forth to eye,   *skirts*
20   As new rewards of her old secrecie!
       What though she hath won on Trust, as many doe,
          And that her truster feares her? Must I too?
       I never stood for any place: my wit
          Thinkes it selfe nought, though° she should valew it.   *if*
25   I am no States-man, and much lesse Divine;
          For bawdry, 'tis her language, and not mine.
       Farthest I am from the Idolatrie
          To stuffes° and Laces, those my Man° can buy.   *fabrics/manservant*
       And trust her I would least, that hath forswore
30   In Contract twice, what can shee perjure more?
       Indeed, her Dressing some man might delight,
          Her face there's none can° like by Candle light.   *but can*
       Not he, that should the body have, for Case
          To his poore Instrument, now out of grace.
35   Shall I advise thee *Pucell?* steale away
          From Court, while yet thy fame hath some small day;°   *influence*
       The wits will leave you, if they once perceive
          You cling to Lords, and Lords, if them you leave
       For Sermoneeres: of which now one, now other,°   *another*
40   They say you weekly invite with fits o' th' Mother,
          And practise for a Miracle; take heed
       This Age would lend no faith to *Dorrels* Deed;
       Or if it would, the Court is the worst place,

---

8 **Epicæne**: epicene, having the characteristics of both sexes
14 **Doth . . . sense**: spends more effort on style than on substance
23 **I . . . place**: I never was a candidate for any position (at court)
29–30 **that . . . twice**: the circumstances are unknown; perhaps these were betrothal contracts
32 **Her . . . light**: alluding to the maxim that all women are attractive by candlelight
33–34 **he . . . grace**: a dismissed former lover who still wishes to encase his instrument in her body
39 **Sermoneeres**: Jonson coined this word for Puritan clergymen, noted for their lengthy sermons; he frequently accused them of lechery
40 **fits . . . Mother**: hysteria, with a pun on making her a mother
41 **Miracle**: exorcism of the hysteria, with a play on virgin birth (see lines 43–46)
42 ***Dorrels* Deed**: the Puritan preacher John Darrel practiced exorcism in the 1590s; he was imprisoned for imposture in 1599

Both for the Mothers, and the Babes of grace,
45 For there the wicked in the Chaire of scorne,
Will cal't a Bastard, when a Prophet's borne.

[U-64]   *An Epigram.*
To our great and good K. CHARLES *On his*
Anniversary Day. 1629.

How happy were the Subject! if he knew
  Most pious King, but his owne good in you!
How many times, live long, CHARLES, would he say,
  If he but weigh'd the blessings of this day?
5 And as it turnes our joyfull yeare about,
  For safetie of such Majestie, cry out?
Indeed, when had great *Brittaine* greater cause
  Then° now, to love the Soveraigne, and the Lawes?   *than*
When you that raigne, are her° Example growne,   *Britain's*
10   And what are bounds to her, you make your owne?
When your assiduous practise doth secure
  That Faith,° which she professeth to be pure?   *the Church of England*
When all your life's a president° of dayes,   *precedent, pattern*
  And murmure cannot quarrell at your wayes?
15 How is she barren growne of love! or broke!°   *broken down*
  That nothing can her gratitude provoke!
O Times! O Manners! Surfet, bred of ease,
  The truly Epidemicall disease!
'T is not alone the Merchant, but the Clowne,
20   Is Banke-rupt turn'd! the Cassock, Cloake, and Gowne,
Are lost upon accompt!° And none will know   *in the reckoning*
  How much to heaven for thee, great CHARLES, they owe!

---

44 Mothers ... grace: mothers claiming impregnation through grace (that is, miraculously) and their babies
U-64.title *Anniversary Day*: the anniversary of his ascension to the throne, 27 March 1625; the poem reflects throughout the political and religious unease of Charles's arbitrary rule (without calling Parliament), which had begun that year, with Jonson upholding the king's position
5 turns ... about: under the Julian or Old Style calendar, still used in England in Jonson's day, the year began on Ladyday, 25 March
10 what ... owne: reflecting the principle that the sovereign is as much bound by the laws as his subjects are
17 O ... Manners: Cicero's famous phrase (in *contra Catiline* 4.190) indicting the evil times and customs that caused the Romans to submit to the cruel rule of Catiline; here used to chastise the English for rebelling against what Jonson believes to be the king's just and good actions (particularly in his role as Supreme Head of the Church)
19 Clowne: peasant, low-born person
20 Banke-rupt: here, morally bankrupt; **Cassock ... Gowne**: here representing the priest, the courtier, and the scholar, respectively

76

[U-70] *To the immortall memorie, and friendship of that noble paire,*
       Sir LUCIUS CARY, *and* Sir H. MORISON.

        The Turne.
    Brave Infant of *Saguntum,* cleare
    Thy comming forth in that great yeare,
    When the Prodigious *Hannibal* did crowne
    His rage, with razing° your immortall Towne.   *leveling*
5 Thou, looking then about,
    E're thou wert halfe got out,
    Wise child, did'st hastily returne,
    And mad'st thy Mothers wombe thine urne.
    How summ'd° a circle didst thou leave man-kind   *summed up, perfected*
10 Of deepest lore, could we the Center find!

        The Counter-turne.
    Did wiser Nature draw thee back,
    From out the horrour of that sack,
    Where shame, faith, honour, and regard of right
    Lay trampled on; the deeds of death, and night,
15 Urg'd, hurried forth, and horld°   *hurled*
    Upon th'affrighted world:
    Sword, fire, and famine, with fell° fury met;   *cruel, fierce*
    And all on utmost ruine set;
    As,° could they but lifes miseries fore-see,   *such that*
20 No doubt all Infants would returne like thee?

        The Stand.
    For, what is life, if measur'd by the space,°   *length*
    Not by the act?°   *accomplishment*
    Or masked man, if valu'd by his face,
    Above his fact?°   *deed*
25 Here's one out-liv'd his Peeres,
    And told° forth fourescore° yeares;   *counted/eighty*
    He vexed time, and busied the whole State;

U-70.title LUCIUS ... MORISON: Sir Lucius Cary, second Viscount Falkland (ca. 1610–43), a model nobleman who was to become the leader of an intellectual group in the 1630s and die fighting on the Royalist side in the first civil war; Sir Henry Morison (ca. 1608–29), knighted in 1627; Cary married Morison's sister in 1630; the poem, addressed to Cary, both mourns the early death of Morison and celebrates the friendship of the two young men; it is modeled on the odes of the Greek poet Pindar (ca. 522–442 BC), the heightened tone and complex metrical structure of which Jonson much admired; the three divisions repeated in it (Turn, Counter-turn, and Stand) correspond to Pindar's strophe, antistrophe, and epode
1–8 Brave ... urne: according to Pliny's *Natural History* 7.3, when the Carthaginian general *Hannibal* (3) sacked the Spanish city *Saguntum* (1) in 217 BC, a newborn child, horrified by the soldiers' brutality, returned to its mother's womb
3 Prodigious: amazing, extraordinary, ominous

    Troubled both foes, and friends;
    But ever to no ends:
30 What did this Stirrer,° but die late?   *troublemaker*
    How well at twentie had he falne,° or stood!   *fallen*
    For three of his foure-score, he did no good.

        The Turne.
    He entred well, by vertuous parts,
    Got up and thriv'd with honest arts:
35 He purchas'd friends, and fame, and honours then,
    And had his noble name advanc'd with men:
    But weary of that flight,
    Hee stoop'd in all mens sight
    To sordid flatteries, acts of strife,
40 And sunke in that dead sea of life
    So deep, as he did then death's waters sup;
    But° that the Corke of Title boy'd° him up.   *except/buoyed*

        The Counter-turne.
    Alas, but *Morison* fell young:
    Hee never fell, thou fall'st my tongue.
45 Hee stood, a Souldier to the last right end,
    A perfect Patriot, and a noble friend,
    But most a vertuous Sonne.
    All Offices° were done   *obligations (as patriot, friend, son)*
    By him, so ample, full, and round,
50 In weight, in measure, number, sound,
    As though° his age imperfect might appeare,   *such that even though*
    His life was of Humanitie the Spheare.°   *perfect form, model*

        The Stand.
    Goe now, and tell° out dayes summ'd° up with feares,   *count/filled*
    And make them yeares;
55 Produce thy masse of miseries on the Stage,
    To swell thine age;
    Repeat of° things a throng,   *reiterate, report, celebrate*
    To shew thou hast beene long,
    Not liv'd; for life doth her great actions spell,°   *denote, declare*
60 By what was done and wrought
    In season,° and so brought   *at the proper time*
    To light: her measures are, how well
    Each syllab'e° answer'd,° and was form'd, how faire;   *detail/its purpose*
    These make the lines of life, and that's her ayre.°   *melody, manner*

        The Turne.
65 It is not growing like a tree
    In bulke, doth make man better bee;

Or standing long an Oake, three hundred yeare,
To fall a logge, at last, dry, bald, and seare:°   *withered*
A Lillie of a Day,
70 Is fairer farre, in May,
Although it fall, and die that night;
It was the Plant, and flowre of light.
In small proportions, we just° beauties see: *true*
And in short measures, life may perfect bee.

The Counter-turne.

75 Call, noble *Lucius,* then for Wine,
And let thy lookes with gladnesse shine:
Accept this garland,° plant it on thy head,   *poem, as a poetic garland*
And thinke, nay know, thy *Morison's* not dead.
Hee leap'd the present age,
80 Possest with holy rage,°   *ecstasy*
To see that bright eternall Day:
Of which we *Priests,* and *Poëts* say
Such truths, as we expect for happy men,
And there he lives with memorie; and *Ben.*

The Stand.

85 *Johnson,* who sung this of him, e're he went
Himselfe to rest,
Or taste a part of that full joy he meant
To have exprest,
In this bright *Asterisme:°*   *constellation*
90 Where it were friendships schisme,
(Were not his *Lucius* long with us to tarry)
To separate these twi-
Lights, the *Dioscuri;°*   *the mythical twins Castor and Pollux*
And keepe the one halfe from his *Harry.*
95 But fate doth so alternate the designe,
Whilst that in heav'n, this light on earth must shine.

The Turne.

And shine as you exalted are;
Two names of friendship, but one Starre:
Of hearts the union. And those not by chance
100 Made, or indenture,° or leas'd out t' advance   *contract*
The profits for a time.
No pleasures vaine° did chime,   *empty*
Of rimes, or ryots, at your feasts,

---

81 bright . . . Day: referring to the eternal day of the New Jerusalem, where "there shall be no night" (Revelation 21:25)

79

  Orgies of drinke, or fain'd protests:
105 But simple love of greatnesse, and of good;
  That knits brave minds, and manners, more then° blood.   *than*

     The Counter-turne.
  This made you first to know the Why
  You lik'd, then after, to apply
  That liking; and approach so one the tother,°   *other*
110 Till either grew a portion of the other:
  Each stiled° by his end,°   *appropriately addressed/aim, goal*
  The Copie of his friend.
  You liv'd to be the great surnames,
  And titles, by which all made claimes
115 Unto the Vertue. Nothing perfect done,
  But as a CARY, or a MORISON.

     The Stand.
  And such a force the faire example had,
  As they that saw
  The good, and durst not practise it, were glad
120 That such a Law
  Was left yet to Man-kind;
  Where they might read, and find
  Friendship, indeed,° was written, not in words: *with a play on "in deed"*
  And with the heart, not pen,
125 Of two so early° men,   *such young*
  Whose lines° her rowles° were, and records.   *biographies/registers*
  Who, e're the first downe bloomed on the chin,
  Had sow'd these fruits, and got the harvest in.

[U-88]   [A Fragment of Petronius Arbiter.]

  Doing, a filthy pleasure is, and short;
  And done, we straight° repent us of the sport: *immediately*
  Let us not then rush blindly on unto it,
  Like lustfull beasts, that onely know to doe it:
5 For lust will languish,° and that heat decay,   *fade away*
  But thus, thus, keeping endlesse Holy-day,
  Let us together closely lie, and kisse,
  There is no labour, nor no shame in this;
  This hath pleas'd, doth please, and long will please; never
10 Can this decay, but is beginning ever.

U-88.title Petronius Arbiter: the Roman satirist (died ca. 66), author of *Satyricon*; the fragment Jonson translates is actually not by Petronius but was attributed to him in a 1585 Paris edition of his works

Prefaced to
MR. WILLIAM SHAKESPEARES COMEDIES, HISTORIES, & TRAGEDIES.

[S-2] To the memory of my beloved,
The AUTHOR
MR. WILLIAM SHAKESPEARE:
AND
what he hath left us.

To draw no envy *(Shakespeare)* on thy name,
   Am I thus ample° to thy Booke, and Fame: *copious, abundant (in words)*
While I confesse thy writings to be such,
   As neither *Man,* nor *Muse,* can praise too much.
5 'Tis true, and all mens suffrage.° But these wayes   *consent, opinion*
   Were not the paths I meant unto thy praise:
For seeliest° Ignorance on these° may light,   *simplest/these opinions*
   Which, when it sounds at best, but eccho's right;
Or blinde Affection, which doth ne're advance
10   The truth, but gropes, and urgeth all by chance;
Or crafty Malice, might pretend this praise,
   And thinke to ruine, where it seem'd to raise.
These are, as° some infamous Baud, or Whore,   *as if*
   Should praise a Matron. What could hurt her more?
15 But thou art proofe against them, and indeed
   Above th'ill fortune of them, or the need.
I, therefore will begin. Soule of the Age!
   The applause! delight! the wonder of our Stage!
My *Shakespeare,* rise; I will not lodge thee by
20 *Chaucer,* or *Spenser,* or bid *Beaumont* lye
A little further, to make thee a roome:
   Thou art a Moniment, without a tombe,
And art alive still,° while thy Booke doth live,   *as yet, always*

S-2: this is the second of Jonson's tributes to Shakespeare in the posthumous first folio publication of the latter's plays (1623); the first is a ten-line poem "To the Reader" facing the engraved portrait of Shakespeare on the titlepage

20 *Chaucer* ... *Beaumont*: all three poets are buried in Westminster Abbey in what is now called the Poets' Corner; Jonson is here countering the first four lines of William Basse's widely circulated "Epitaph upon Shakespeare": "Renowned *Chaucer* lie a thought more nigh / To rare *Beaumond*; and learned *Beaumond* lie / A little nearer *Spencer,* to make roome / For *Shakespeare* in your threefold fourefold tombe"; Shakespeare was buried in Holy Trinity Church in Stratford-upon-Avon

        And we have wits to read, and praise to give.
25   That I not mixe thee so, my braine excuses;
        I meane with great, but disproportion'd° *Muses:*   *not comparable*
        For, if I thought my judgement were of yeeres,°   *for all times*
        I should commit thee surely with thy peeres,
        And tell, how farre thou didst our *Lily* out-shine,
30   Or sporting *Kid,* or *Marlowes* mighty line.
        And though thou hadst small *Latine,* and lesse *Greeke,*
        From thence to honour thee, I would not seeke
        For names; but call forth thund'ring *Æschilus,*
        Euripides, and *Sophocles* to us,
35   *Paccuvius, Accius,* him of *Cordova* dead,
        To life againe, to heare thy Buskin° tread,   *boot, representing tragedy*
        And shake a Stage: Or, when thy Sockes° were on,   *representing comedy*
        Leave thee alone, for the comparison
        Of all, that insolent *Greece,* or haughtie *Rome*
40   Sent forth, or since did from their ashes come.
        Triúmph, my *Britaine,* thou hast one to showe,
        To whom all Scenes of *Europe* homage owe.
        He was not of an age, but for all time!
        And all the *Muses* still were in their prime,
45   When like *Apollo* he came forth to warme
        Our eares, or like a *Mercury* to charme!
        Nature her selfe was proud of his designes,
        And joy'd to weare the dressing of his lines!
        Which were so richly spun, and woven so fit,
50   As,° since, she will vouchsafe no other Wit.   *that*
        The merry *Greeke,* tart *Aristophanes,*
        Neat *Terence,* witty *Plautus,* now not please;
        But antiquated, and deserted lye
        As° they were not of Natures family.   *as if*
55   Yet must I not give° Nature all: Thy Art,   *assign to*
        My gentle *Shakespeare,* must enjoy a part.
        For though the *Poets* matter,° Nature be,   *subject matter*

29–30 *Lily* ... **line**: three of Shakespeare's contemporaries; **Lily**: John Lyly (ca. 1554–1606), author of the prose romance *Euphues* and prose comedies; **Kid**: Thomas Kyd (ca. 1557–ca. 1595), author of *The Spanish Tragedy,* one of the bloodiest and most popular plays of the time (Jonson is making a joke on his name in calling Kyd **sporting**); **Marlowes mighty line**: the poet and playwright Christopher Marlowe (1564–1593) was often commended for the power of his blank verse
33–34 *Æschilus* ... *Sophocles*: the three great Greek tragic poets of the fifth century BC
35 *Paccuvius* ... *Cordova*: three ancient Roman writers of tragedy; **him of Cordova**: Seneca
44–46 *Muses* ... *Mercury*: all three were associated with the arts
51 *Aristophanes*: greatest of the ancient Greek writers of comedy
52 *Terence* ... *Plautus*: renowned ancient Roman writers of comedy
56 gentle: perhaps alluding to the fact that after becoming wealthy through part ownership of his theater, Shakespeare bought a coat of arms and thereby became a "gentleman"

       His Art doth give the fashion. And, that he,°   *man*
       Who casts° to write a living line, must sweat,   *intends, undertakes*
60   (Such as thine are) and strike the second heat
       Upon the *Muses* anvile: turne the same,
          (And himselfe with it) that he thinkes to frame;
       Or for° the lawrell,° he may gaine a scorne,   *instead of/laurel wreath*
          For a good *Poet's* made,° as well as borne.   *crafted (by study)*
65   And such wert thou. Looke how the fathers face
          Lives in his issue, even so, the race°   *children*
       Of *Shakespeares* minde, and manners brightly shines
          In his well torned,° and true filed° lines: *turned/polished*
       In each of which, he seemes to shake a Lance,
70   As brandish't at the eyes of Ignorance.
       Sweet Swan of *Avon!* what a sight it were
          To see thee in our waters yet appeare,
       And make those flights upon the bankes of *Thames,*
          That so did take° *Eliza,* and our *James!*   *captivate*
75   But stay, I see thee in the *Hemisphere*
          Advanc'd, and made a Constellation° there!   *Cygnus, the swan*
       Shine forth, thou Starre of *Poets,* and with rage,
          Or influence, chide, or cheere the drooping Stage;
       Which, since thy flight from hence, hath mourn'd like night,
80   And despaires day, but° for thy Volumes light.   *except*

                                                BEN: JONSON.

---

66 issue: here, his plays, with a play on their now being "issued" in full in print
69 shake ... Lance: a play on Shakespeare's name; Shakespeare's coat of arms reflects the same wordplay, displaying an armored hand shaking a spear
74 bankes ... Thames: Shakespeare's theatre, the Globe, was on the south bank of the Thames
74 Eliza ... James: Queen Elizabeth I and King James I, both of whom held Shakespeare's plays in high regard
80 Volumes: volume's, referring to the first folio of his plays, to which this poem is prefaced

Index of Titles and First Lines

Titles are entirely in capital letters, first lines in mixed capitals and lower case. Lengthy titles are shortened by ellipsis. Titles beginning with "A," "AN," or "THE" are alphabetized under the first significant word.

After many scornes like these, (U-2.3)
And must I sing? what subject shall I chuse? (F-10)
ANOTHER LADYES EXCEPTION PRESENT AT THE HEARING (U-2.10)
At court I met it, in clothes brave enough, (E-11)
Away, and leave me, thou thing most abhord (E-65)

BEGGING ANOTHER, ON COLOUR OF MENDING THE FORMER (U-2.7)
Brave Infant of *Saguntum,* cleare (U-70)

CAMDEN, most reverend head, to whom I owe (E-14)
A CELEBRATION OF CHARIS IN TEN LYRICK PEECES (U-2)
Charis guesse, and doe not misse, (U-2.6)
Charis one day in discourse (U-2.8)
CLAYMING A SECOND KISSE BY DESERT (U-2.6)
COB, thou nor souldier, thiefe, nor fencer art, (E-69)
Come my CELIA, let us prove, (F-5)

Doing, a filthy pleasure is, and short; (U-88)
Do's the Court-Pucell then so censure me, (U-49)
Drinke to me, onely, with thine eyes, (F-9)

AN ELEGIE (U-22)
AN ELEGIE (U-38)
AN ELEGIE (U-40)
AN ELEGIE (U-41)
AN ELEGIE (U-42)
AN EPIGRAM ON THE COURT PUCELL (U-49)
AN EPIGRAM. TO ... K. CHARLES ON HIS ANNIVERSARY DAY ... (U-64)
AN EPISTLE ANSWERING TO ONE ... SEALED OF THE TRIBE OF BEN (U-47)
EPISTLE TO ELIZABETH COUNTESSE OF RUTLAND (F-12)
EPISTLE. TO KATHERINE, LADY AUBIGNY (F-13)

EPITAPH ON ELIZABETH, L.H. (E-124)
EPITAPH ON S.P. A CHILD OF Q. EL. CHAPPEL (E-120)
EPODE (F-11)
Ere cherries ripe, and straw-berries be gone, (E-92)

False world, good night: since thou hast brought (F-4)
Farewell, thou child of my right hand, and joy; (E-45)
Fine MADAME WOULD-BEE, wherefore should you feare, (E-62)
Follow a shaddow, it still flies you; (F-7)
For his Mind, I doe not care, (U-2.10)
For *Loves*-sake, kisse me once againe, (U-2.7)
[A FRAGMENT OF PETRONIUS ARBITER] (U-88)

Good, and great GOD, can I not thinke of thee, (F-15)

Heare mee, O God! (U-1.2)
HER MAN DESCRIBED BY HER OWNE DICTAMEN (U-2.9)
HER TRIUMPH (U-2.4)
Here lyes to each her parents ruth, (E-22)
HIS DISCOURSE WITH CUPID (U-2.5)
HIS EXCUSE FOR LOVING (U-2.1)
How blest art thou, canst love the countrey, WROTH, (F-3)
How happy were the Subject! if he knew (U-64)
HOW HE SAW HER (U-2.2)
How I doe love thee BEAUMONT, and thy *Muse,* (E-55)
A HYMNE ON THE NATIVITIE OF MY SAVIOUR (U-1.3)
A HYMNE TO GOD THE FATHER (U-1.2)

I beheld her, on a Day, (U-2.2)
I doe but name thee PEMBROKE, and I find (E-102)
I know to whome I write: Here, I am sure, (U-14)
I now thinke, Love is rather deafe, then blind, (U-9)
I sing the birth, was borne to night, (U-1.3)
If all you boast of your great art be true; (E-6)
If, my religion safe, I durst embrace (E-95)
If *Rome* so great, and in her wisest age, (E-89)
INVITING A FRIEND TO SUPPER (E-101)
It will be look'd for, booke, when some but see (E-2)

JEPHSON, thou man of men, to whose lov'd name (E-116)

Kisse me, sweet: The warie lover (F-6)

Let it not your wonder move, (U-2.1)
Let me be what I am, as *Virgil* cold (U-42)

MADAME, had all antiquitie beene lost, (E-105)

May none, whose scatter'd names honor my booke, (E-9)
May others feare, flie, and traduce thy name, (E-17)
Men that are safe, and sure, in all they doe, (U-47)
MY PICTURE LEFT IN SCOTLAND (U-9)

THE NEW CRIE (E-92)
Noblest *Charis,* you that are (U-2.5)
Not to know vice at all, and keepe true state, (F-11)
Now that the harth is crown'd with smiling fire, (F-14)

O Holy, blessed, glorious *Trinitie* (U-1.1)
ODE. TO SIR WILLIAM SYDNEY, ON HIS BIRTH-DAY (F-14)
Of your Trouble, *Ben,* to ease me, (U-2.9)
Oh doe not wanton with those eyes, (U-4)
ON GILES AND JONE (E-42)
ON LIEUTENANT SHIFT (E-12)
ON LUCY COUNTESSE OF BEDFORD (E-76)
ON MY FIRST DAUGHTER (E-22)
ON MY FIRST SONNE (E-45)
ON POET-APE (E-56)
ON SIR VOLUPTUOUS BEAST (E-25)
ON SOME-THING, THAT WALKES SOME-WHERE (E-11)
ON SPIES (E-59)
ON THE UNION (E-5)

PLAY-WRIGHT me reades, and still my verses damnes, (E-49)
POEMS OF DEVOTION (U-1)
Poore POET-APE, that would be thought our chiefe, (E-56)
Pray thee, take care, that tak'st my booke in hand, (E-1)

Retyr'd, with purpose your faire worth to praise, (E-126)
ROE (and my joy to name) th'art now, to goe (E-128)

See the Chariot at hand here of Love (U-2.4)
SHIFT, here, in towne, not meanest among squires, (E-12)
Since you must goe, and I must bid farewell, (U-41)
THE SINNERS SACRIFICE. TO THE HOLY TRINITIE (U-1.1)
Some act of *Love's* bound to reherse, (F-1)
A SONG (U-4)
SONG. THAT WOMEN ARE BUT MENS SHADDOWES (F-7)
SONG. TO CELIA (F-5)
SONG. TO CELIA (F-9)
SPIES, you are lights in state, but of base stuffe, (E-59)

That Love's a bitter sweet, I ne're conceive (U-40)
That *Poets* are far rarer births then kings, (E-79)
This morning, timely rapt with holy fire, (E-76)

87

Thou art not, PENSHURST, built to envious show, (F-2)
Thou, that mak'st gaine thy end, and wisely well, (E-3)
Though Beautie be the Marke of praise, (U-22)
'Tis growne almost a danger to speak true (F-13)
'Tis true, I'm broke! Vowes, Oathes, and all I had (U-38)
TO ALCHYMISTS (E-6)
TO ALL, TO WHOM I WRITE (E-9)
To draw no envy *(Shakespeare)* on thy name, (S-2)
TO EDWARD ALLEN (E-89)
TO ELIZABETH COUNTESSE OF RUTLAND (E-79)
TO FINE LADY WOULD-BEE (E-62)
TO FRANCIS BEAUMONT (E-55)
TO HEAVEN (F-15)
TO HIS HONORD FRIEND MR JOHN SELDEN (U-14)
TO HIS LADY, THEN MRS. CARY (E-126)
TO JOHN DONNE (E-96)
TO KING JAMES (E-35)
TO MARY LADY WROTH (E-105)
TO MY BOOKE (E-2)
TO MY BOOKE-SELLER (E-3)
TO MY MEERE ENGLISH CENSURER (E-18)
TO MY MUSE (E-65)
To night, grave sir, both my poore house, and I (E-101)
TO PENSHURST (F-2)
TO PERTINAX COB (E-69)
TO PLAY-WRIGHT (E-49)
TO ROBERT EARLE OF SALISBURIE (E-43)
TO SICKNESSE (F-8)
TO SIR HENRIE SAVILE (E-95)
TO SIR HENRY NEVIL (E-109)
TO SIR ROBERT WROTH (F-3)
TO SIR WILLIAM JEPHSON (E-116)
TO SUSAN COUNTESSE OF MONTGOMERY (E-104)
TO THE IMMORTALL MEMORIE ... OF ... CARY, AND ... MORISON (U-70)
TO THE MEMORY OF ... MR. WILLIAM SHAKESPEARE ... (S-2)
TO THE LEARNED CRITICK (E-17)
TO THE READER (E-1)
TO THE SAME (F-6)
TO THE WORLD. A FAREWELL FOR A GENTLE-WOMAN ... (F-4)
To thee, my way in *Epigrammes* seemes new, (E-18)
TO WILLIAM CAMDEN (E-14)
TO WILLIAM EARLE OF PEMBROKE (E-102)
TO WILLIAM ROE (E-128)

URGING HER OF A PROMISE (U-2.8)

Weepe with me all you that read (E-120)
Were they that nam'd you, prophets? Did they see, (E-104)
WHAT HEE SUFFERED (U-2.3)
What need hast thou of me? or of my *Muse?* (E-43)
When was there contract better driven by *Fate?* (E-5)
While BEAST instructs his faire, and innocent wife, (E-25)
Whil'st that, for which, all vertue now is sold, (F-12)
Who now calls on thee, NEVIL, is a *Muse,* (E-109)
Who sayes that GILES and JONE at discord be? (E-42)
Who shall doubt, DONNE, where I a *Poet* bee, (E-96)
Who would not be thy subject, JAMES, t'obay (E-35)
Why, *Disease,* dost thou molest (F-8)
WHY I WRITE NOT OF LOVE (F-1)
Would'st thou heare, what man can say (E-124)

MRTS

MEDIEVAL & RENAISSANCE TEXTS & STUDIES
is the publishing program of the
Center for Medieval and Early Renaissance Studies
at the State University of New York at Binghamton

MRTS emphasizes books that are needed —
texts, translations, and major research tools.

MRTS aims to publish the highest quality scholarship
in attractive and durable format at modest cost.